God and Humanity
at Marshall

God and Humanity at Marshall

Toward November 14, 1970, and Beyond

Mark Coppenger

RESOURCE *Publications* · Eugene, Oregon

GOD AND HUMANITY AT MARSHALL
Toward November 14, 1970, and Beyond

Resource Publications
An Imprint of Wipf and Stock Publishers
199 W. 8th Ave., Suite 3
Eugene, OR 97401

www.wipfandstock.com

PAPERBACK ISBN: 978-1-7252-8129-5
HARDCOVER ISBN: 978-1-7252-8130-1
EBOOK ISBN: 978-1-7252-8131-8

Manufactured in the U.S.A.   09/04/20

Contents

Contents

Contents

Preface

September 8, 2012, I was in the Metropolitan New York Baptist Association (SBC) building, teaching an extension course for Southern Baptist Theological Seminary in Louisville. On that Saturday, the association was celebrating its twenty-fifth anniversary in their Upper West Side building with a picnic in Central Park. As it happened a powerful storm hit the city at the same time, with heavy winds and rainfall driving the participants several blocks west to the shelter of the building.

We'd just broken for lunch and witnessed the influx of a crowd of more-or-less-soaked Baptists, who set out their food for an indoor picnic. I found myself seated beside Dwain Gregory, a man about my age (in his sixties), and we began to get acquainted. When I learned he was director of Baptist Student Ministry at West Point, I told him I'd played the same role at Wheaton and Northwestern, and then he added that he'd also held that position at the Air Force Academy and Marshall University. Hearing this latter name, I recalled the horrific plane crash that took out the football team, and he told me that he was there in those days, adding that a revival of sorts had occurred in its aftermath. (We also had occasion to talk in subsequent years, first at West Point, after I'd attended his Sunday School class with cadets, and later in a Manhattan restaurant.)

When I'd heard a bit of the story, I said he should write it up, and he agreed, having been told that before. But he didn't count himself much of a writer, so I said that maybe I could help. Sure enough, before long, I found myself in Huntington, stopping there on a trip from the East Coast to Louisville, talking to Alan Wild, whose name came up through a contact Dwain suggested.

Wild was happy to pitch in, and he began to describe a fresh work of God on campus, but not the one Dwain described. Rather, Wild's story concerned the summer and fall before the crash. At first, I was a little disappointed that he didn't build on Dwain's account, but rather opened up another narrative. The story was becoming more complex.

As I pursued it, one source would recommend another and then others would branch from that, and the branches were spreading wide. After talking with Dwain and Alan, I decided the account needed to cover the entire 1970–1971 school year, but that was soon upset by Gregg Terry, who pointed me to strong activity in 1967. And then, on another trip, I had supper with Pastor Reggie Hill and his wife, who were eager to tell me of the strong Christian presence and witness of players in the 1990s. And by that time I had discovered Christianly-rich items in the Special Collections of the Marshall University library, and my original paradigm gave way to a new one—the spiritual history of Marshall University, albeit with focus on the late twentieth century, and special attention to the year of the crash.

For a title, I've drawn from two things: 1. William Buckley's 1951 classic, *God and Man at Yale*, and 2. the May 6, 1937 radio account of the fiery, Hindenburg crash, where station WLS's Herb Morrison exclaimed, in horror, "Oh, the humanity!" Like Buckley, I hope to offer an informative (and yes, perspectival) account of the spiritual life of the school. And I want to give special attention to the terrible event that "put Marshall on the map," not only for the loss and subsequent triumphs, but also for the continuing reflections, many of them edifying, on the event.

We've seen the film, *We Are Marshall*, which centered on the football program—its personalities, its tragedy, its comeback. And, within the film, we glimpsed a spiritual aspect of the moment, with a scene shot in the chapel of the Campus Christian Center. But there is a broader story to be told.

Saying that, I have to add that this small book just scratches the surface, but I hope it helps to alert the reader to the great role that faith, indeed, Christian faith, has played and will continue to play in the life of Marshall University. It began as a small project in devotional writing, but grew to encompass a range of phenomena both inspiring and depressing, items inviting commentary, both positive and negative. Being a philosopher/theologian, I philosophize/theologize a bit; being a preacher, I preach a bit—and all from a conservative, evangelical standpoint, the only one I have.

So this book has been built in layers, starting with an inspirational core (concerning manifestations of God's work around the time of the crash), building out as a chronicle of the school's record in the spiritual realm (with generous help from the school's archivists), and layering critical observations on what I've found along the way (whether positive, negative, or mixed). Admittedly, it's an ungainly concatenation, guaranteed to both please and displease most everyone who reads it. But it's my take on the matter at this juncture. And I trust that a good many people (perhaps student ministers, pastors, coaches, athletes, professors, administrators, parents, legislators, or jurists) might find something useful here, whether in stirring the heart, informing the mind, steeling the will, or building community.

I wish that the national coronavirus shutdown (including Marshall's) had not coincided with the last months of work on this manuscript. In some cases, photocopied dates are fuzzy and a range of double-checks and supplemental inquiries have been stymied. But, thanks to those who so generously supplied their time and assistance, I've had enough to press ahead with a good deal of the story in the fiftieth-anniversary year of the tragedy that pierced so many hearts and prompted my study.

Acknowledgements

Special thanks go to the dozen figures who granted me interviews, their names cited throughout the book and to the Special Collections staff under the direction of archivists Nat DeBruin and Lori Thompson, who provided me most generous access and assistance. I'm also glad that the bookstore maintains a range of books and videos covering the 1970 tragedy with its ripples. On my eleven trips to Huntington and the university, I've enjoyed nothing but helpfulness. And a word of gratitude is due to SBTS student David Closson who downloaded and printed out the hundreds of images I garnered with my cell phone camera from the Marshall archives. (I say emphatically that none of those cited in this book are responsible for its failings, for these are surely my own.)

As always, I could not have managed without the wonderful patience and encouragement of my wife Sharon, who indulged (and sometimes accompanied me on) my forays into West Virginia, who prayed for my work on this book, and who painstakingly worked through the manuscript with me, addressing mechanics as well as substance.

And again, thanks to Dwain Gregory, pictured here in his Marshall days and then in one of our three meetings.

Dwain Gregory, *The Parthenon*,
March 18, 1971, Marshall University
Special Collections.

Dwain Gregory, New York City, May 8, 2014

Introduction

What's in a Namesake—Marshall?

A GOOD MANY BOOKS chronicle the work of God on Christian college campuses. One thinks, for example, of J. Edwin Orr's *Campus Aflame*,[1] covering "evangelical awakenings in collegiate communities" on such avowedly Christian schools as the Congregationalists' Yale under Timothy Dwight in 1802, the Baptists' Baylor and non-denominational Wheaton in the 1930s, and the Methodists' Asbury, whose 1970 revival is chronicled in Robert Coleman's book, *One Divine Moment*.[2] To be sure, Orr also covered the work of God on secular campuses, as at the University of Michigan in 1858, where ripples from the New York City prayer revival spread throughout the Midwest. But the dynamics are different, in that the administration is on board at religious schools, while on secular campuses, the administrators are observers rather than official agents of awakening. And, indeed, this tracks with America's First Amendment stance against *state* establishment of religion (but not with the current conceit that the state should be hostile toward religion in its institutions).

There is a healthy tension there, one that is captured in the life of Marshall University's namesake. For though not avowedly Christian himself, John Marshall was amiably disposed toward the faith and did not shrink from association with believers. He was the fourth Chief Justice of the Supreme Court and was supremely instrumental (through his opinion in the case of *Marbury v. Madison*) in instituting the practice of "judicial review." As distinguished a figure as Marshall was, the school's naming was something of a happenstance. In 1837, citizens in the small community of Guyandotte, then a part of Virginia, decided they needed a school for their children. So they met in the home of lawyer, John Laidley, to draw up plans, and he suggested the name of his late friend, the Chief

Justice. They agreed, so it became Marshall Academy, operating as a "subscription school" in the Mount Hebron Church, a log structure used by a number of congregations through the years. It operated under Virginia charter until it was closed by the Civil War. Then, in 1867, it gained a charter from the new state of West Virginia, and was now designated as the State Normal School of Marshall College.

Though John Marshall, having died in 1835, had no inkling that there would be a West Virginia school named in his honor, or perhaps even that there would be a West Virginia, his life provides something of a template as we reflect on the special relation between public education and religious devotion. The First Amendment of the Constitution specifies a distinction between state and church, guaranteeing the free exercise of religion while proscribing its establishment by government authorities. Years later, Thomas Jefferson put his stamp on this interpretation by saying, in a letter to some Baptist pastors in Danbury, Connecticut, that there should be a "wall of separation" between the two, and since World War II, the courts have addressed the question of whether such a wall is truly constitutional, and if so, how porous that wall should be.

In comparing John Marshall with Thomas Jefferson, Jean Edward Smith said, "They each abstained from organized religion (Jefferson more outspokenly) . . ."[3] In Marshall's case, his parents did little to encourage the faith:

> Despite the occasional presence of a parson in the house, or the fact that Mary Randolph Keith was the daughter of a minister, piety and religious dogma played little role in the education of the Marshall children. Thomas Marshall and his wife were church members, but they made little attempt to inculcate their beliefs. Instead, the children were encouraged to think for themselves. Senator Humphrey Marshall openly scorned religion; Dr. Louis Marshall confessed agnosticism; and brothers James and Thomas were notably devoid of religious sentiment. John Marshall never rejected the church openly, but his acceptance was environmental rather than doctrinal. Throughout his life the chief justice declined to become a member of any congregation, unable to believe in the divinity of Christ. If Marshall needed reinforcement for that skepticism, it may have come from Pope. *The Essay on Man* is a ringing endorsement of the deist views of the *Age of Reason*, and although Pope was a Catholic, his emphasis on man as a rational being inevitably diminished the role of Christianity.[4]

So, though Marshall's upbringing did not encourage devotion to Christ, it did foster respect for the church:[5]

> Later that December [in 1811], tragedy struck Richmond when the city playhouse, jammed with a holiday audience, went up in flames, killing seventy people and injuring over a hundred. Marshall had not attended the theater that evening, but he rushed to the scene to help fight the fire and rescue those who could be saved. The following day he was named to head a committee to raise funds for a memorial to the victims, a project that culminated in the building of Richmond's Monumental Church on the site of the former theater. Marshall, though he did not belong to the church, and though he had difficulty accepting the divinity of Christ, nevertheless purchased a pew near the chancel and attended regularly. For the chief justice, it was a matter of "setting a good example" for his friends and neighbors, rather than a reflection of devout faith.[6]

Two sides to the man. And there are two sides to Marshall University, reflecting more or less and in various ways, the free (and often energetic) exercise of faith and its non-establishment as school policy.

Endnotes

1. Orr, *Campus Aflame*.
2. Coleman, *One Divine Moment*.
3. Smith, *John Marshall*, 12.
4. Smith, *John Marshall*, 36.
5. We should note that Justice Marshall was a high officer in a quasi-religious organization, as grand master of the Grand Lodge of the Ancient Free and Accepted Masons of the state of Virginia.
6. Smith, *John Marshall*, 406.

In Loco Parentis

As NOTED ABOVE, MARSHALL Academy first met in 1837 as a "subscription school" in the Mount Hebron Church, a log structure used by a number of congregations through the years. Charles Hill Moffatt (longtime history professor and a senior deacon at Huntington's Fifth Avenue Baptist Church) recounts the denominational connections with the institution's founding:

> Financial support for the school was obtained, not only from the Methodist settlers in the valley, but also from the Presbyterian farmers, who agreed to help finance the academy if they might be privileged to worship in the chapel of the school. Since this arrangement was agreeable to the founders, it obviated the need for the Presbyterians to travel ten arduous miles to attend the church of their faith on the other side of the river in Burlington, Ohio.[1]

Then, in 1838, the Virginia legislature (before Virginia and West Virginia were separate), adopted the academy. Closed by the Civil War, it reopened in 1867 (now in West Virginia) as the State Normal [teachers] School of Marshall College.

The Clothed Public Square

Though Marshall became a state school in the late 1860s, it had no notion that the Constitution required, in the words of Richard John Neuhaus, a "naked public square,"[2] where religious speech was anathema. On the contrary, Christian religious talk was everywhere to be found, yet not oppressively so, as reflected in this wording from the 1871–1872 catalogue:

This institution being designed to serve the interests of all classes in the state, is and almost always must be unsectarian. All forms of private religious convictions will be respected. But while the sectarian part of religion is held in abeyance, sound morality and those great principles of revealed religion upon which all sects are substantially agreed will receive due attention. The highest type of character is the intelligent Christian; to this all students will be urged to aspire.

This statement was tweaked in the 1887–1888 catalogue, with wording common in the catalogues throughout the closing years of the nineteenth century. It ended not by speaking of the high character of intelligent Christians, but by saying that the neglect of these moral and religious principles and forces would result in "disastrous failure."

That being said, we read, under the heading, "Moral and Religious," that "No student of immoral character is allowed to remain in the school." Furthermore,

The daily work of the school is begun by religious exercises, upon which every student, unless specially excused, is required to attend. The different religious denominations have their churches, pastors and Sunday Schools in the city, and these are means of good influence on the student.

The 1897–1898 catalogue celebrates the institution of chapel, saying, "The attendance on, attention to, interest and unity of effort in, and reverence for, the chapel exercises have been a source of great satisfaction to us, indicating, as it seemed, a very high order of moral and religious tone among the students." Though chapel always concluded with the Lord's Prayer and included sacred songs along with the secular, the school was unapologetic in making it compulsory for all students. Furthermore, the school was at work identifying "at least 100 scriptural readings for responsive exercise" for the upcoming year.

"Decently and In Order"

In writing about the conduct of worship, the Apostle Paul concludes chapter fourteen of 1 Corinthians with the admonition, "Let all things be done decently and in order." It tracks with the school's concern that students and teachers know and respect standards of decorum, focus, and industry, with attendant sanctions should behavior not measure up. It also reflects the way in which the Bible prescribes salutary comportment according to universal principles of right versus wrong, of civility versus rudeness, of stewardship versus indolence. While Scripture is quite "sectarian" regarding the way of salvation (as in the Five Solas of the Reformation), it offers many general teachings on right conduct and attitude. Of course, Proverbs is full of wise counsel, as are such lists as the Ten Commandments in Exodus and the contrasting manifestations of flesh and Spirit in Galatians 5:19–26. Furthermore, Romans 1 and 2 help explain why Christians and non-Christians alike can agree on a moral code, since some behaviors are manifestly unnatural and repugnant (1:26–27), with these observations backed by ethical impressions on the heart (2:14–15). Theologians call this "general revelation" (which complements the "special revelation" of Scripture), enabling our grasp of "natural law," which undergirds "common sense." Thus, the state-funded Marshall did not shrink from honoring the contribution of the Bible to campus programs and order.

When it published "Rules for the Government of Pupils" in the 1880–1881 catalogue, it insisted on conduct perfectly consonant with biblical ideals and, indeed, encouraged by the teachings of Scripture, e.g., "All defacement of the walls, seats, desks, or other property of the School, is prohibited," and "Care of clothing, books and person is enjoined on students." Lame, post-hoc, excuses for missing class (e.g., "Not hearing the bell . . . being out late the preceding evening . . . mislaying books or articles of apparel) were disallowed. And if infractions occurred, demerits followed, e.g., five for "improper or profane language" and one for "talking or whispering in study room." Ten demerits in one month prompted an "admonition from the Principal," and it went up from there. Accountability also extended beyond the campus, as with the declaration, "Students are forbidden to visit any place where intoxicating drinks are sold as a beverage," with suspension or dismissal as live options. Whatever the shady venue or departure from the right path, the school declared, "We expect our students to be ladies and gentlemen, and to be studious, or at once withdraw from school" (1899–1900).

(This was a more restrained approach to discipline than that employed by James Beauchamp Clark, the school's twelfth principal (1873–1874): "When faced with a hazing incident by four students, one of whom refused to apologize, Clark gave him the option of apologizing, of being expelled, or he said, 'I will thrash you with[in] an inch of [your] life.'" (The student took option #1.)[3]

In laying out the system of demerits, the first presupposition was, "All government of men and women that is not self-government is not only un-American, but unnatural." This is an extraordinary claim. First, to clarify, "self-government" means "self-control" or "self-discipline," and not "democracy." On this interpretation, one can read "unnatural" as "hypocritical" or "forced, and not the outworking of genuine character." That's a disputable claim, in that hypocrisy comes quite naturally to many. On the other hand, if "natural" means, "conducive of well-being," then the claim is more plausible, for purely-compelled behavior is not easily sustainable. But the use of "un-American" is most interesting. One supposes it means that people regimented by totalitarians are less admirable than Americans, whose choices are not dictated by despots.

Building on this notion, the 1887–1888 catalogue states, "There is no government worthy of the name, that has not for its basis *self government*. There is especial need for the application of this principle in a Normal School—a school of teachers, for he who can not govern himself will not succeed in governing others."

The 1897–1898 catalogue extends the rules to professors: "Manifestation of anger in class is NEVER justifiable in teacher or student" and "In direct proportion as the teacher instills a spirit of self-control by inspiriting high ideals of decorum, the need of discipline disappears." (Incidentally, the 1876–1877 catalogue proscribed, on penalty of expulsion, "Striking, in anger, any pupil or teacher . . ."). Furthermore (as in the 1889–1890 catalogue), Marshall encouraged "tattling" in the interest of enforcement, for "if the truth be an offense against [the] school," then it is "noble." Indeed, "concealing it is a crime, and the concealer is morally PARTICEPS CRIMINIS ["a partner in crime"]."

"A Word to Parents"

The 1897–1898 catalogue assures parents:

> Though there are moral snares for the young in all cities and large towns in excess of those encountered in the country and in villages, (and Huntington is no exception), still, under the regulations of this school, children are as safe here as anywhere, and have the advantages of culture not found in smaller places and in rural districts. The boarding place of every student is known to, and must be approved by, the faculty. All changes in boarding places are

reported, also. We make it a point to note carefully the associations of every student in and out of school, and, as soon as regarded questionable, the principal calls attention to it. Inquiries are made of those who board students, concerning their company, their student hours, sleep hours, and other matters deemed important to the faculty to know. This method of looking after the welfare of students not in the dormitory—the place where every lady student who does not live in the city should, for many reasons, board—will be more fully systematized during the year 1898–99, when not only must every boarding place be approved by the faculty, but blank reports will be furnished the hostess who keeps board-ers, which must be filled out and returned to the principal every Saturday. These reports will contain all needed information about the students under her charge, such as hours of study, recreations, sleep, and deportment about the house.

The school also aspired to build character, as when, in the 1899–1900 catalogue, it pressed male students to take on summer work in Huntington to help pay for their education. Such was a sign of "true manhood." And it demeaned finicky eating: "Good, substantial food, students must have. Delicacies are WHOLLY unnecessary."

In that same catalogue, in "A Word to Parents," the university wrote:

It is a pleasure to receive your sons and daughters and to assume any reasonable responsibility you may elect to transfer to us while your child is under our direction. We are glad to act as purser, purchaser, guardian, and instructor, if in so doing you will encour-age those whom you enter as students to WORK. We believe in work. We regard it as the best to safeguard known to youth or age, against bad habits, failure, misfortune, or sorrow—the only sure means of promotion, of substantial growth, and of genuine success. We must insist that those who come here, study, and study much. We have never discovered any remedy for indifference, idleness, and stupidity, but labor; and when we have failed to have a student work we regard his place at home and not at school and we shall send him there; this, however, not till we have tried every remedy at our command.

"Necrology"

In the 1899–1900 catalogue, the "Necrology" (obituary) section mentions God in connection with the deaths in the Marshall community, e.g., a teacher, Laura Sandige, who, at age 26, was struck with a fever and "quietly withdrew, as a member in good standing, not only from this school, but from that part of God's unknown universe which we, for want of a better term, call 'the world.' " She was deemed "conscientious, quick to observe, attentive to duty, respectful to authority, very kind in her school relations, in all things and at all times the same careful, industrious, Christian lady." Her entry concluded that we "bow the head in silence to reflect upon the inexplicable 'whys' of the Infinite , then go our several ways again, better if we are wise enough to learn wisdom from God's instruction through nature's lessons." And then, a student, Benjamine Blaine, who died of typhoid fever at twenty-two, was remembered with a poem beginning, "Man is a being whereof God is the dream . . ."

The Racial Context

Despite institutional concern for moral rectitude, the school, the state, and, indeed, the nation suffered from a blind spot characteristic of the Jim Crow Era. That failing is reflected in this entry from the 1897–1898 catalogue. Under the heading, "Social and Religious," we read

> In this city are thirteen churches for white people, some of them splendid edifices, handsomely finished and furnished, and ALL have good congregations. The denominations are: M.E. Church, 2; M. E. Southern, 2; Baptist, 2; Presbyterian, 1; Christian, 1; Catholic, 1; Jewish, 1; United Brethren, 1; Congregational, 1; Episcopal, 1. These churches extend a most cordial welcome to our students to attend all their exercises.

Incidentally, the 1917 yearbook, *Mirabilia*, noted that long time teacher James W. Samples (pictured with long white beard) "served in the Confederate Army during the Civil War," adding "Hats off to the man with grit enough to face the hard tasks of school life after passing the age of activity for most men."

2

The Y Years

As the twentieth century dawned, Marshall continued with its unabashed profession of concern for the spiritual lives of its students. The 1900–1901 catalogue lists "board" at around $10 a month, assuring inquirers, "In this we are excelled by no place offering the same social, religious, and other culture which Huntington offers." It goes on to assure prospects, regarding "The Spirit of the School," that

> Without boast or semblance of self praise,—for that is farthest from our motive—the very atmosphere about the college is such that evil-doing, lagging, and recklessness are almost impossible. The spirit that pervades the student body is one of very great respect for authority, reverence for things sacred, and consideration for the comforts and rights of others.

Granting talk of reverence for things sacred, that same catalogue makes it clear that Marshall is not a denominational or sectarian school, insisting that ethics would be taught from a neutral standpoint, using the nineteenth-century text by Frederick Ryland, wherein "Right, justice, equity, goodness, and other ethical principles are treated from the civic rather from the religious point of view. The Platonian idea of developing and training for citizenship in a Republic is made the central thought, ethics being a civic and not a religious study."

Huntington's Religious Opportunities

Nevertheless, in President Woodley's era (1915–1919), a sign on the bulletin board in College Hall warned women, "If you don't go to church today you can't go anywhere today."[4] And, indeed, church attendance was urged for both men and women. In a catalogue note "To Parents," the school encouraged them to contact local ministers—Baptist, Methodist Episcopal, Congregational, Presbyterian, Brethren, Catholic, Jewish—for "unbiased information" regarding the churches, the city, and the school. Furthermore, the student body was well engaged with Huntington religious events. For instance, on December 15, 1921, *The Parthenon* gave front-page coverage to a series of Bible lectures by G. Campbell Morgan, held in the city auditorium and hosted by the Federation of Women's Missionary Societies, the Association of Women's Clubs, and the Ministerial Association. To large crowds, including a "mass choir drawn from the city's churches," the guest spoke on "The Bible—Some Reconsiderations"; "The Historic Christ—A Study of the Records"; and "Some Superlative Sayings of Jesus: The Church of God According to the Teachings of Christ."

The Y

Such was the continuation of themes adopted by nineteenth-century Marshall, but there were strong, fresh, spiritual developments on campus, most notably in the emergence of YMCA and YWCA chapters. Founded in London in 1844, the Young Men's Christian Association was designed to provide spiritual and social nurture for young men who'd flocked to the cities in connection with the Industrial Revolution. Through Bible study and prayer, the YMCA helped these displaced folks from the country cope with the physical and moral squalor of their new surroundings. The Y found its way to Boston in 1851, and, in 1856, the first student chapter was established at Cumberland University in Lebanon, Tennessee, then a Baptist school.

A sister group, the Young Women's Christian Organization, began as an outgrowth of other movements in England and developed throughout the latter decades of the nineteenth century. In 1894, the world organization (including Great Britain, the U.S., Norway, and Sweden) was formalized. In America, the name YWCA was first used in Boston, and the first student group was established in Normal, Illinois, in 1873.

By the turn of the century, Marshall had its own chapters, with E. Garland Ray and Laura E. Wallace listed as presidents of their respective groups in the 1900–1901 yearbook. Both Y's continued strong on campus on into the 1920s, with yearbook photos of the era showing as many as forty-two members in the YMCA and fifty-four in the YWCA, a considerable portion of the student body, which then numbered just over a thousand.

Today, we think of physical fitness when we hear someone say they're going to the Y, and certainly that was part of program from the early years, but there was a pointedly Christian aspect to the organization back then. For one thing, the YMCA was quite active spiritually among the soldiers in the European theater during World War I, with a massive effort heralded by such luminaries as President Woodrow Wilson, General John Pershing, and Supreme Allied Commander, Marshall Foch. (Incidentally, the Marshall chapter contributed $100 to Belgians who were suffering under the German army.)[5]

Though it offered a wide range of welfare and recreational services, boosting soldier morale and effectiveness, the "C" in YMCA was unmistakable. It was reflected in a letter from Robert P. Wilder, head of the Y's Bureau of Religious Work to "camp secretaries" serving stateside on military posts where troops were preparing for deployment. He prescribed these objectives:

1. To lead men to Christ.

2. To keep professing Christians loyal to their Lord.

3. To relate all who come under the Association's influence to the principles and aims of the Kingdom of God.[6]

And though soldiers were not pressed to sign the Y's War Roll card, 326,311 did so, affirming, "I hereby pledge my allegiance to the Lord Jesus as my Saviour and King, and by God's help will fight His battles for the victory of His Kingdom." The soldier kept a tab as a reminder, and the card was forwarded to the Y's Religious Work Bureau, which notified relatives and home churches.[7]

Though the Y espoused Christ, it wasn't narrowly doctrinal or exclusionary in its ministry. Within the Christian fold, one communion service was held for eleven hundred men with members of forty different denominations present. Indeed, the mix of other religions could be complex, as at Long Island's Camp Upton, housing draftees from New York City's Lower East Side: "A census of the camp at one time showed men of sixty-one forms of faith, including Catholics, Jews, Protestants, in that numerical order, followed by a scattering of Free Thinkers, Mormons, Mohammedans, Theosophists, Holy rollers, Confucianists . . ." Consequently, the Y workers began to form alliances with other groups, finding "common ground on which all could work together."

In this connection, an "Inner Circle" arose, sponsored by the YMCA, Knights of Columbus, and Jewish Welfare Board. Her members signed off on the following:

> Having answered my country's call, and recognizing that an obligation rests on me, as a member of the National Army, to be a strong and efficient soldier, and realizing the need of help in meeting this obligation, I do hereby pledge myself to cooperate with other like-minded men by forming in my barracks an Inner Circle which will promote the following: 1. Clean thinking; 2. Clean Speech; 3. Clean Living; 4. Character Building. (Character is formed through prayer, Bible study, attendance on divine worship, and service for other men.)[8]

Tracking with the military program of the Y, the missions arm was avowedly Christian, with an ecumenical cast, congruent with their theme verse, John 17:21—"That they all may be one; as thou, Father, art in me, and I in thee, that they also may be one in us: that the world may believe that thou hast sent me." In this evangelistic context, we read a report in *The Parthenon* on one campus meeting, noting, "The President was fortunate enough to have just received a letter from Miss Stienbach, our missionary in China, which was read and thoroughly enjoyed." Also, the 1926 yearbook listed, among the committee chairs, Opal Lawson for Bible and Wade Burdette for Missions, and the 1927 yearbook shows Walter Long as the chair of the Deputation Committee, concerned with helping students gather support for their mission ventures. In this spirit, the Y held international parties, with the participants wearing the dress of various nations, such as Holland, Japan, and India.[9]

Of course, foreign missions was not their only focus. In the March 26, 1926 *Parthenon*, we read of the Marshall Y's domestic "extension work":

> Teams composed of from three to five men each, are visiting weekly the small churches in the outlying districts from Huntington, including villages in Ohio. The nature of the work consists in giving talks concerning religion and similar topics, and in furnishing music. Last week a team was sent to Bradrick, Ohio, where church

services were held in the absence of the regular pastor. Usually, the places to be visited by the "y" have no minister at all.

On campus, the programs were more wide ranging, covering not only Christianity (or religion in general for that matter), but also topics of basic morality and decency more typical of the four values listed on the Inner Circle card. Usually, the two Y's would meet separately. For instance, the YMCA alone heard Professor Hedrick speak on Leo Tolstoy's notion of peace, while the YWCA alone heard a Mrs. Lehnhoof (student secretary of Southern Home Missions for the Methodist Church South) on the theme, "Come—Abide—Follow." But they could come together for a joint session, as when they assembled to hear the YMCA sponsor, Dr. White, address the topic, "Who Is My Neighbor?" And sometimes they fielded a panel, such as the one appointed in 1924 by White to discuss "What is God?" "Shall We Accept the Bible as Infallible?" and "What is the Value of Prayer." (The second topic was particularly pertinent to the Fundamentalist-Modernist Controversy that arose in the 1920s.)

Throughout the term, programs and speakers were quite varied, with, for instance, one semester featuring:

- Rev. J. Layton Mauze, pastor of the First Presbyterian Church, on "Russia"
- Dr. Edward Phelps, professor of chemistry, on "Science and Religion"
- Edward West on "Christian Faith"
- Rabbi A. Feinstein of the Jewish Temple on the "Jewish Conception of Jesus"
- Professor Lee A. Wolfard of the business administration department on "Success in Business"
- Professor L. J. Corbly, former president of Marshall, on "Life at its Best"
- Rev. Fred W. Hagan of First Congregational Church on "A Broad Religion"
- Ray Walker leading a discussion on "Christian Influence"
- Dr. Morris P. Shawkey, president of Marshall, on "College and Christianity"
- And Dr. A. S. White, Y advisor, on "Marshall College and the Y.M.C.A."

On another occasion, Rabbi Feinstein spoke on prejudice:

Ninety-five per cent of our lives is shaped by prejudice. There is no absolutely unprejudiced mind. Nations build emotional walls and fences between each other and so create fear and hatred. If we are ever to approach the ideal of international friendliness—if we are ever to lead moral lives we must destroy these walls of prejudice. I would persuade you to submit your prejudices to the light of the truth. Everywhere prejudice is poisoning the hearts of men, and most prejudice is caused by ignorance. Prejudice is either the result of ignorance, or lazy-mindedness or a tendency to follow the mob. It takes mental courage to be an individual. An individual must think for himself and be guided by his conscience. To master our prejudices there are three steps necessary. We must begin with ourselves—we must learn to love the truth as we see it—and we must refrain from passing dogmatic judgment. Always seek the truth. Let it be one aim of your life to root prejudice from your life and to plant in its stead love for truth. Dare to think for yourself. Such are to be the saviors of our sick and suffering world.

Then Chief Redfox St. James of the Blackfoot Indians told the assembly:

The laws of the Indians, incorporated in a Decalogue as in other civilizations, include a law of health, of labor, of education, of hospitality, of kindness, of motherhood and fatherhood, of sanctity of body, of self-restraint, and of immortality. All Indians do not have hooked noses or high cheekbones. Many of the younger Indians have a lighter skin. Indians have gone through Harvard and Yale. We believe in progress. Let the pipe of peace be smoked between the red man and the white man, and let the flag of peace wave over this, your adopted land and the land of my fathers.

At the close of meetings, they would typically sing the 1915 "Mizpah" hymn, by C. Harold Lowden: "The Lord watch between thee and me . . . while we are absent one from the other."

As admirable as the Y's may be today, their focus is a far cry from that of their founders, but this is not surprising. Without a clear doctrinal statement, a confession of faith, the organization has evolved (or devolved) into a society concerned with generic goodness and fitness, but such was not the case in those opening decades of the twentieth century, whether at Marshall or abroad.

(As a postscript, the October 18, 1933, issue of *The Parthenon* reports the resignation of Professor L. J. Corbly, who'd been advisor to the group "with honor and student approbation since its organization" at Marshall. The headline read, "Corbly Cites Reasons for Y Resignation; Suggests Y's Are

Often Dominated by Cliques; Believes Groups Have Lost Hold; Feels Days of Y.M.'s Effective Good in College Ended." The student president, Evert Hines, also resigned, mentioning the fact that the organization was deep in debt. As for the YMCA, *Parthenon* coverage continued strong into 1935.)

The Naismith Connection

In 1891, on two weeks' notice, James Naismith invented a game involving tossing balls into suspended peach baskets, and the world has not been the same since. At the Basketball Hall of Fame in Springfield, Massachusetts, James Naismith's New Testament is on display, along with this legend, written under "Spirit":

> As a student and teacher at Springfield's YMCA, James Naismith was immersed in a theological school of thought known as Muscular Christianity. Muscular Christianity was a theological perspective that emerged in the mid-nineteenth century that celebrated physical exertion, comradeship and determination and emphasized manliness, virility, morality, health, and patriotism. Further, physical activity and sports developed character and instilled Christian values and ethics that would serve the participants throughout their life. For Naismith, sports was the training ground for spiritual development and moral awareness. Naismith saw basketball as a way to keep young men involved in healthy activity and to inculcate them with the Christian values for which the YMCA stood. Naismith insisted that basketball should be put "on such a basis that it will be a factor in the molding of character as a recreative and competitive sport." In short, basketball would enable young men to fulfill the promise of the three components of the YMCA's emblem and creed symbolized by the YMCA's Red Triangle, the mind, body, and spirit, into the whole person.

Thanks to the Y, this new game would go international in short order, with amazing results. As we read in *Operation Yao Ming*, the Houston Rockets of the NBA would be the beneficiary of a "breeding program" initiated by Mao Zedong, traceable back to Naismith's work for the Y in Massachusetts:

> One of the YMCA's fastest-growing missions at that time happened to be China, then a land of four hundred million that was opening up to Western religions. Over the next few years after Naismith's invention, dozens of missionaries would set off for the mysterious

Middle Kingdom, their rucksacks packed with Bibles and "The 13 Rules of Basketball." A century later, global visionaries at Nike and Reebok would look at China's massive population and dream about all the soles to be sold. But at the end of the nineteenth century, the YMCA saw China as the world's biggest market for souls to be saved. And in their eyes, salvation would come through God and sports, although not necessarily in that order.[10]

Reformers were keen on the game, for it advanced their program of modernization by leading young men away from "the most humiliating symbols of emasculated feudalism: the long gowns, fingernails, and ponytails that form part of the imperial court's traditional dress."[11] Furthermore,

The YMCA's emphasis on athletics as a way of fostering self-reliance, moral rectitude, and national pride resonated in a society wary of more dogmatic evangelical appeals. By 1920, the organization had more foreign missionaries in China than anywhere else in the world, and it operated athletic centers in all of the country's major cities. Basketball became a mainstay among urban youth, as migrants and missionaries soon carried the game to the vast rural interior. In 1935, the sport was officially declared a national pastime.[12]

One of the Y coaches asked when China might be able to field a winning team at the Olympics, but the problem was clear—the Chinese teams lacked sufficient height to compete—so the government got involved. It scoured the countryside, looking for tall men and women and then encouraged them to marry. And, indeed, in due season, they produced the seven-foot, six-inch Yao Ming in Shanghai as well as another NBA player, the seven-foot Wang Zhizhi.

Meanwhile, back in the U.S., basketball found its way to Marshall, where the school paper encouraged student spectators to behave themselves:

Don't criticize the referee—he likely knows more than you do.

Don't "ride" the opposing team.

Don't hoot and yell when they are shooting free throws: It usually doesn't affect their accuracy, anyhow, and it is poor sportsmanship.

Don't wait till your team is ahead before you cheer; help them to get ahead.

Speaking of good manners, *The Parthenon* held a "courtesy contest," convinced that, "In the building of a character in a democracy, there is perhaps no trait as indispensable as common courtesy." It explained that special recognition should go to those who "expressed inner thoughtfulness by outward graciousness." It's not clear how they monitored and measured this throughout the student body, but their heart was in the right place.

Life Service Club

The Y wasn't the only campus organization pointing toward the ministry and missions. The 1921 yearbook, *Mirabilia*, records that on March 7, a Life Service Club was organized. ("All students planning for definite Christian work are eligible for membership.") Among the generous descriptions of the graduating seniors in that same yearbook, we read of Erville Ellis Sowards from Fort Spring, West Virginia—a very active student, with time on the inter-collegiate debating team, a member of several groups (Choral; Cercle Français; Classical; Athletic Board, and yes, the YMCA), and editor of both the yearbook and the school paper (*The Parthenon*). At the close of his entry, we read:

> When he leaves us, Marshall will lose one of the most efficient students that ever entered her portals. Yes, we would not call him back because the life of service that he has begun here will be continued in a foreign land where he goes to the Light that has helped him over so many rough places. He is now under appointment by the American Baptist Foreign Mission Society to sail the coming summer for Rangoon, Burma, where he will do educational work in the high schools, preparing students for Judson College.

Such references to spiritual orientation and activity were commonplace in those years. An early *Mirabilia* says of Eva Sandige (not to be confused with the aforementioned, departed, Laura Sandige), "She is a loyal member of the C.E.C. and Y.W.C.A." Similarly, the 1914 *Excelsior* notes that Emma Bell Turney "will sing a song of gladness when we are glad, and a song of cheer when we are discouraged, for dear to God and to man is sacred song."

Chapels, Vespers, etc.

Schoolwide chapel continued on into the twentieth century with this explanation in the 1900–1901 catalogue for The State Normal School:

Twenty to thirty minutes are set apart for these exercises each day, usually beginning at TEN O'CLOCK. All students are expected to be present. The worship, consisting of two or three sacred songs, scriptural readings, a short extemporaneous prayer or the concert offering of the Lord's prayer, sometimes both, are found objectionable neither to our Catholic students, of whom we have quite a number, nor to those who affiliate with no church. To believer and disbeliever alike these exercises are regarded as morally healthful, orthodoxically unobjectionable, socially beneficial, and spiritually profitable.

These chapel gatherings were a mixture of the sacred and the secular, perhaps better called assemblies or convocations. For instance, the first chapel for the 1921 school year featured the West Virginia superintendent of schools, who said the legislature, in an effort to raise standards, had been generous in budget allocations. The speaker for the second chapel was a Dr. Jenkins from Johnson Memorial Church, who offered a "stimulating and helpful talk," which left them feeling like Ulysses, determined "to strive, to seek, to find, and not to yield." That same fall, the Armistice Day Convocation focused on an arms conference in France, "the final hope of the nations of the earth," thus the campus's "desperate prayer for the success of the meeting." One "chapel" was given to the home economics department for their play, "The Home Economics Extravaganza Dinner." Another to Dr. S. L. Roberts, who urged students, "Find a way to solve your difficulties," using the example of Dr. Russell H. Conwell, who managed to climb up to an eagle's nest, where others had failed. (The Kiwanis Club Chorus provided the music.)

A November chapel gathering heard F. W. Hagan of the Congregational church, who used Luke 5 for his text ("Launch out into the deep and let down your nets"). He applied it to the admonition that they do more than simply go to church, but also cooperate with others for good works out in the community. ("The impressive service was closed with a prayer.") Later, Rev. Mr. Goodwin of the Methodist church drew on the Mark 12:17 ("Render unto Caesar . . .") and "illustrated his talk by a short but vivid review of 'Hunger,' by Knut Hamsun, a recent Nobel prize winner." Furthermore, chapel was not limited to Christian clergy. For instance, the aforementioned Rabbi Feinstein told them that the supreme purpose of a college education was "to develop the capacity to think independently," adding that "it is far more glorious to be a seeker after truth than to actually possess it."

Not everyone was thrilled with chapel. For one thing, assigned seating separated women from men. For another, those who found it boring formed a Chapel Skippers Club in 1917, only to have some members called before "the Pope in the Vatican" (President Woodley) for "counsel."[13]

The college also featured vespers, and the March 26, 1926 *Parthenon* reported on two messages delivered at this gathering. Reverend R.W. Miles, university secretary of the Southern Presbyterian Church, said,

> No education worthy of the name is complete without religion, and no religion has adequate preparation without education. Religion and education should go hand in hand . . . There never was a time that, in the history of America, college students have thought so much about religion as today. If you talk about religion, you are in line with the other students and with the thinking people of America. Religion is now a vital question . . . Reality cannot be explained, but it can be acted. Christianity has more actable truth than anything else in the world. The church is the agency through which to work. If you must criticize the church, do it from the inside in a constructive manner.

Another speaker, the aforesaid Dr. White, observed,

> If the Bible is what many people insist it is, it would be well for us to know more about it. If it is the inspired word of God, the creator of the universe, we ought to go to it to learn our weaknesses . . . Christ in the wilderness faced decision, and through this wilderness, every young man and every young woman must go if they are to amount to anything. We must decide whether our success shall reside in the material realm, or whether our lives shall be devoted to the spiritual. We can attain spiritual altitudes if we are willing to wrestle with the problems.

Furthermore, Christian themes worked their way throughout the campus, as when the Training School staged a play honoring the Pilgrims and the Junior Secondary Class held a Christmas party. In a 1920 article on "Christmas Spirit," we read, "We are thrilled with the spirit of giving and 'peace on earth and good will to all mankind' the kind of peace that passeth understanding. Like the old hymn 'Old Time Religion,' it makes us love everybody."

Guest lectureships also contributed to the religious teaching of the school, e.g., one by Rabbi Stephen S. Wise, the international Zionist leader and minister of the Free Synagogue in New York City, and the Japanese evangelist, Tsurin "Paul" Kanamori, who spoke on "American-Japanese Relations."[14] (Kanamori was called "the Dwight Moody of Japan" and was renowned for his three-hour sermon on "God, Sin, and Salvation," preached eight hundred times to a total of three hundred thousand people.)[15]

Bible Parodies

The 1917 yearbook offered a couple of takeoffs on familiar biblical texts. This one's signed off with "M. H." (Though the writer despairs of a future in entomology, a career in literature seems promising.):

Twenty-Third Psalm

1. Mr. LeCato is my teacher; I shall not pass.

2. He maketh me to remember the names of many bugs; He leadeth me to expose mine ignorance before the class.

3. He maketh me draw grasshoppers' pictures on the board for my grade's sake;

4. Yea, tho I try forever, I shall catch no bugs; for cocoons are hard to see, and live worms badly frighten me.

5. He asketh me questions in the presence of mine classmates, my answers he does not like; My grade runneth under.

6. Surely bugs and "D's" shall follow me all the days of my life; And I shall dwell in the class of Entomology forever.

In the same volume, this writer works from the opening chapters of the Bible:

Genesis 1–12

1. In the beginning, MR. WOODLEY created a new atmosphere around Marshall College. 2. The boys and girls walked thru the halls together, and words of love were upon the tongues of all. 3. He spoke unto the teachers and said: "Let there be change," and there was a change . . . 6. And he said: "Let those who talk in chapel be gathered together unto the front seats and let their voices roll unto the skies"; and it was so. He divided those who ought to be in the library and study hall from those in class; and those who were in neither place were called to the office . . . 8. MR. WOODLEY called this *Discipline*, and it grieved us sorely . . .

Cringe-Inducing Jokes

Some of their activities make us wince today. In the 1916 *Mirabilia* under "The Minstrel," we read that that year's show was "bigger and better than ever before. Instead of a single row of singers and one blackface on each end, there were two rows of the chorus and three burnt cork comedians making faces at one another." The next page covers a production of *The* [Black] *Wedding*, wherein "the most entertaining of pickaninnies sang, 'Aunt Malindy's Wedding Day,' while a jovial preacher took his place in the pulpit."

And both the campus newspaper and the yearbook printed jokes of the day. Some were harmless:

> Daisy: "Before Australia was discovered what was the largest island in the world?"
>
> Evah: "I don't know."
>
> Daisy: "Australia, wasn't it?" (1921)
>
> She was only a taxidermist's daughter, but she knew her stuff. (1929)

But some were embarrassingly crude, such as these from the 1929 yearbook:

> Medical Examiner (to alien, who has just landed): Say, don't you ever bathe?"
>
> Alien: "I never came to America before."
>
> A man may marry a broad without going to Europe.
>
> Son: "What's the difference between angels and fairies?"
>
> Dad: "Well, angels are very pure and sacred, while fairies are queer creatures."

An early *Mirabilia* analogizes Pentecost (reported in Acts as the occasion when the Holy Spirit came upon the Church, an event marked by the miraculous comprehension of the Apostle Peter's sermon in the various languages of those present). In summing up the record of graduating senior, St. Elmo Fox, they write that "the number of languages she can command reminds one of the day of Pentecost and the gift of tongues." Confidence in making this connection was grounded in a common knowledge of the Bible characteristic of that era. However, those who came to identify themselves as Pentecostals didn't fare so well in the joke department. The 1919 yearbook served up this unfortunate piece:

His Mistake

"You still wish to join?"
"Sure!"
"You realize that your throat may be torn open?"
"Sure!"
"Your chest torn asunder and your heart torn out?"
"Sure!"
"That your leg may be torn off?"
"Sure!"
"And your body torn in two?"
"Sure!"
"Knowing all this, you still wish to join the Holy Roller Church?"
"Holy Roller meetin'!" I thought youse was organizin' a Marshall football team!"

So they had a way to go on sensitivity.

Excuse Me, Ma'am

Jokes weren't the only problem. The 1914 *Excelsior*, a special publication for the graduating class, said of Mertie Backus of Poe, West Virginia, ". . . In classes, too, she is a star, never failing to recite when called on. In spite of the fact that her sunny smiles are impartially distributed among the Marshall lads, we predict that she will not join the ranks of 'old maid school teachers' but will settle down to the quiet duties of the home." And of Ruth Donovan of Huntington, ". . . She is an excellent student, which makes her popular with all her teachers, especially Mr. Franklin . . . She is acquiring widespread fame by her graceful dancing ability for attracting the opposite sex. She hopes to become an A. B. but we fear she will end by becoming an "M R S."

In that same publication, a line of verse described one of teachers with

Miss Hawkins took a course in Art
That she might some day win fame;
Then she taught in the public schools
And had never yet changed her maiden name.

In that same extended poem, typifying faculty members one by one, we find reference to the women's vote, whose ratification through the Nineteenth Amendment was six years away:

Miss Doyle was a suffragette,
She made some splendid speeches,
And said that men would do just right
If they practiced what she preaches.

And then there was the 1911 *Mirabilia* entry on graduating senior, Lucy Thomas of St. Albans:

Miss Thomas is one of the quiet retiring girls who, nevertheless, manages to have a good time. She is one of the Jolliest girls in the Dormitory and the girls always welcome her as a visitor. One of her particular pleasures is a geology field trip on cold rainy days. She is well acquainted with the way a certain professor makes love and any girls wishing to be enlightened on this subject may call at Room No. _____ College Hall.

Well, the meanings of expressions can very well change through the years.

3

"Fundamentalism" vs. "Modernism"

SOME ARGUE THAT WORLD War I prompted a sea change in American culture, with loosened sexual standards and an increasing impatience with the counsel of the Bible. Hence the song, "How You Gonna Keep 'Em Down on the Farm (After They've Seen Paris)?" which featured such lyrics as "wine and women play the mischief, with a boy who's loose with change!" and "How ya gonna keep 'em away from Broadway? Jazzin' around, and painting the town? How ya gonna keep 'em away from harm? That's the mystery."

The Fundamentals and the Social Gospel

Of course, this was just one stream of influence reshaping American culture in the opening decades of the twentieth century. A host of nineteenth-century German scholars (including Wellhausen, Baur, Schleiermacher, Strauss, and Feuerbach) had used "higher criticism" to cast doubt upon the historical, theological, and moral reliability of the Bible, and their perspective was insinuating itself into American seminaries and churches. In 1922, at New York's First Presbyterian Church, ordained Baptist minister, Harry Emerson Fosdick preached a sermon, "Shall the Fundamentalists Win?"—a fiery retort to those who were espousing the "Fundamentals" against perceived slippage in Christian orthodoxy. Reprinted as "The New Knowledge and the Christian Faith," the sermon was sent to a hundred and thirty thousand pastors, the enterprise funded by John D. Rockefeller Jr., son of the founder of Standard Oil.

The fundamentals in question (popularly identified as 1. an inspired, infallible Bible; 2. the virgin birth; 3. the atoning death of Christ; 4. the bodily resurrection of Jesus; and 5. the reality of Jesus's miracles) were defended in a multivolume set of essays distributed to a quarter million church leaders around 1920. These essays were penned by a wide range of scholars, including college and seminary professors (at Oberlin, Wycliffe, Knox, McCormick, Reformed Episcopal, Xenia Presbyterian, Southwestern Baptist, Moody, Princeton, Southern Baptist, and Biola) as well as pastors, bishops, editors, attorneys, denominational officers, and parachurch leaders. And it was this movement—its leaders and constituency alike—to which Fosdick was responding. (Incidentally, funding for this publication and its distribution came from the founders of another energy corporation, Union Oil, today's Unocal.)

About that same time—prominently in the person of Walter Rauschenbusch—a "social gospel" was arising, one which said the church had neglected to free people from hell on earth in its efforts to get people into heaven. But its advocates, in their zeal for social reform and relief of the downtrodden, tended to shortchange the message of soul salvation, either ignoring it or substituting a salvation by good works. And so other battle lines were drawn.

Though President Shawkey was demonstrably conservative on a number of fronts, he was pleased to invite the theological luminary, Shailer Mathews, dean of the University of Chicago Divinity School, to speak at one of the commencements. Wishing to "go after the big guns" for "the big event of the year," he did, indeed, gain a big one in Mathews.[16] Mathews was a leading light of the "social gospel" movement and a devotee of biblical "higher criticism" (impatient with the "biblical inerrancy" of the man in the pew). Though he helped start the Northern Baptist Convention and served as its president in 1915, his ashes are buried in the First Unitarian Church of Chicago.

The Scopes Trial

Of course, the most prominent event in this conflict was the Scopes Trial in Dayton, Tennessee. With the publication of Charles Darwin's *The Origin of Species* in 1859, skeptics had found a compelling alternative to the creation story in Genesis 1 and 2, and many Christians felt the need to accommodate Darwinism, espousing some form of theistic evolution, whereby God used the machinations of natural selection to bring forth man. This conflict came to a head in 1925, when an East Tennessee science teacher was persuaded to test the law against teaching evolution, and Chicago lawyer Clarence Darrow was enlisted to defend him, with the prosecution in the hands of William Jennings Bryan. (Bryan had been a Congressman, Secretary of State, and a frequent candidate for President.)

Bryan won the case, but at great cost to the creationists, for Darrow was widely hailed as the intellectual victor, with Bryan as the champion of rubes. (Arthur Miller later penned the drama, *Inherit the Wind*, to enforce, with artistic license, this take on things.)

Under President M. P. Shawkey (1923–1935), Marshall took up the issue in a number of connections. Shawkey argued both for the superiority of the Bible and against concerns that Darwinism conflicted with it. In an address to a vespers gathering, he said, "Christianity is, I believe, the best interpretation of the best innate religious feeling of man. The Bible has been given us as a torch to light the way." In the spring of 1926, at a vesper's service, he spoke of its three revelations:

> [1] The Bible is a higher conception of religious truth than is found anywhere else in the world. The imperfection of science at that time and the fragmentary history contained in the Bible have sometimes led to a misunderstanding of the inspired word, but if we go on we will find the real purpose of it is pretty plain after all. It is only in the nonessentials that people disagree . . . [2] The second revelation is the conflict between geology and the history recorded in the Bible. Geology is proof of the revelation of the book. The persistence of life in cycles and the indestructibilty of matter suggests the story of how life began. [3] Nowhere do we find a group of people who do not harbor the hope of an eternal life. Life here is tangible, but somewhere man has believed that there is a life more extensive than this. I cannot conceive that there would be a persistent hope without realization. If the human mind were to exist through an immortality without satisfaction, that would be punishment enough. If man is critical, he need not go far to find cooperation in a world where the heavens declare the glory of God. If you can come to the conclusion that you can exist without religion, you are the first one I have found. Paul says "if we have not hope for the future, we are of all men most miserable." Many orthodox churches are accusing colleges of being nonreligious, but most colleges were established by religious people and patronized by religious people more than any others. They are not antagonistic to religion but are the torch bearers of religion as well as of scientific truth. Let your own spiritual nature have a chance to grow and expand itself in acts of good will toward

your fellowman, and you have the best type of religion. The most important thing in our contact of life is with our spiritual nature.

That same spring, as reported in a March 5, 1926 *Parthenon* article, eleven professors were asked to weigh in on the anti-evolution laws recently enacted in some southern states:

- C. E. Hedrick, dean of arts and sciences, said that, in a democracy, the taxpayers of those various states had a perfect right to "decide upon the course of study pursued in their schools."

- Watson Selvage, head of philosophy and psychology, observed, regarding Mississippi, "Considering that all intelligent people supposed that the fight for evolution was won a generation ago, we have a fair index of the mentality of this half-negro community." Among other sweeping and contemptuous things, he added, "Now the question of evolution—so far as it is a question—is a biological question, and is as much a closed question as the binominal theorem. Any scientist who denies them is not a scientist and anyone who sidesteps the issue is a coward, however great his fear of the cackle and intolerance of ignorant people."

- J. B. Shouse, dean of the teachers college, said that, though he wasn't generally in favor of restrictive legislation, he wasn't going to get excited about it, "for the matter will take care of itself." He noted that there had been other explicit or de facto prohibitions, as against sectarian commentary on the Bible, against teaching German during World War I, and against gainsaying the Constitution.

- R. P. Heron [sic], head of physics, opposed such restrictive law since it was counterproductive to tell the specialists what was best for the classroom.

- Edward P. Phelps, associate professor of chemistry, said the evidence for evolution was incomplete but sufficient and that they should be as free to teach it as they do atomic theory and the spherical frame of the earth.

- Dr. Haworth, head of literature, is simply reported as being against such laws.

- Dr. Heitzel, associate professor of English, said, "About two generations ago the theological perplexities which the theory of evolution gave rise to were unraveled to the satisfaction of all thinking individuals . . . To speak of the conflict between religion and belief in evolution shows the speaker confused in his terminology; to revive the discussion even is like fighting over again old forgotten battles. It is true that the idea of evolution may not harmonize with certain unessential beliefs . . . but it does not necessarily have any fundamental bearing on the religion of any man . . The [scientist's] sole business, so far as he is the scientist, is to know the truth. That, I take it, is a worthy ideal; and were his findings to conflict with accepted notions, it may be well to re-examine those notions in the light of the truth-seeker's findings . . . To legislate against evolution is as futile as commanding the hill to come to you . . . The person whom I have been describing is an individual of narrow interests and consequently very limited in his range of thinking. For that reason he should not have the ridicule of those who cannot agree with him, but their pity; not their contempt but their sympathy; not . . . misinformation, but education whenever possible."

- Professor Carl G. Campbell, head of chemistry, noted that prohibition may backfire, for "human nature being what it is, whatever is prohibited will have a certain attraction which is not intrinsic," and it may be advanced "surreptitiously". . . Those who teach such principles of evolutionary development should be careful to avoid being swayed by prejudice and should never be dogmatic in their statements. All we want is the truth, the whole truth, and nothing but the truth."

- H. G. Toole, associate professor history, said the laws were utterly out of synch with the times, for the "prevailing attitude in the modern institutions of learning is one of open-mindedness and tolerance toward the discussion of any idea, theory, or law."

- W. L. Utterback, head of biology, said he thought it perfectly possible for "God-fearing" people to teach the principles of evolution, which are like those of gravity. Furthermore, evolution doesn't entail an account of man's origin, but merely presents an hypothesis which deserves a hearing.

- A. S. White, a doctor of jurisprudence, said, "My objection to the anti-evolution legislation rests on the fact that all legislation in the realm of ideas, whether by king, priest, or legislature, is a denial of the fundamental basis on which all government by the people rests . . . When it comes to legislating ideas out of existence we are trying an experiment that neither king nor pope found successful. Benjamin Franklin once said that those who would give up essential liberty to purchase a little temporary safety deserve neither liberty nor safety."

(Incidentally, President Morris Shawkey (1923–1935) dismissed both Selvage and White in 1927, for he found neither to be a "loyal and constructive type of citizen" and both to be contemptuous of existing institutions. And it didn't help that the Huntington Ministerial Association expressed unhappiness with the theological views of the two professors, that Selvage was "opinionated and offensive" toward those who disagreed with him, and that White was so rude as to habitually read the newspaper in faculty meetings.)[17]

The consensus was, indeed, that Darwin posed no problem for the faith. One headline read

Science Agrees with Bible is H'Ron Verdict
Professor Talks to Y.M.C.A. on Topic of Religion and Science
Christianity is Simple
Plausible Explanations for Apparent Clashes is Point

Another reported on an address to a joint session of the YMCA and YWCA by the prickly Selvage:

Our Religion is Changeable Says Selvage
Can Adjust Itself to Modern Thought and Science Says Prof
Must Make Adjustment
Each Generation Adjusts Itself as It Moves Slowly Ahead

In one student editorial:

> Scientific workers have had some hard knocks lately from misguided people who thought science was hurting religion. To quote an imminent authority, "This was foolish, for if a religion is true, a little more truth can't hurt it, and whatever isn't true isn't science." It was additionally foolish because whatever we think about the next world, science is one of the best friends most of us have in this one. If science hadn't cut the general death rate from 17.6 a thousand in 1900 to between 11 and 12 in 1924, there would have been at least 600,000 more deaths in this country last year than actually took place. This is about 12 times the number of Americans who were killed or died of wounds in the war with Germany.
>
> Prof. Wolford in a recent address to the YMCA made a very fine statement in regard to the relative place of science and religion with which we are in full accord: "True science and true

Christianity," he said, "are complementary each to the other. Man has an intellect; science must train it. Man has a soul, a spiritual self; religion must reclaim, cultivate, and develop it."

Legislators by passing laws cannot prevent revelation of truth nor stop for long the progressive movement of science. They should not seek to do so.

Luther Burbank said the other day that "those who would legislate against the teaching of evolution should also legislate against gravity, electricity and the unreasonable speed of light, and should introduce our clause to prevent the use of the telescope, the microscope, and the spectroscope, or any other instrument of precision which may in the future be invented for the discovery of truth" . . .

Science and religion both have their place in the life of today and the proper cognizance of the seemingly evident fact would greatly benefit a number of American legislators.

In an interesting exchange with that same Professor Wolford, the editor of the *Parthenon* felt obliged to defend himself and the school against the suggestion that there was a lack of appreciation for the faith:

We have yet to hear a single student or faculty member of Marshall College disavow his belief in the matchless teachings of he who in the long, long ago exhorted men to know the truth, for thus only could they become free and enjoy the abundant life of which he spoke so tellingly. We have yet to hear a single student or faculty member of the college deny that the Christ of the Bible and the Christian religion was not [sic] the criterion of true character. To have anyone even hintingly impute before a Christian association that such was not our belief and especially when the accusation is based upon an inference not well taken is something we very keenly resent. Simply because a man desires to dare to think independently for himself rather than accept what James Harvey Robinson terms "the whisperings of the herd" does not mean that he will reject everything or anything that mankind regards as high and holy.

College, in our opinion, is a place where students should at least learn how to think. As a paper the thing that we are primarily interested in is that out from beneath the classic shades of Marshall College should go men and women who are not mere stalking companions and blind and servile worshipers of the status quo, but thinking individuals with an intelligent view of things. If we are wrong in taking such a stand, we will consider anyone who will point out to us the error of our ways as a kind and compassionate friend. Until then we shall continue our present policy.

Utterback

William Irvin Utterback, quoted briefly above, deserves special mention. Marshall historian Charles Moffat was not particularly impressed with his take on the issue:

> In the Biology Department William I. Utterback was an interesting, though somewhat bizarre scientist, whose publication, entitled Fresh Water Mussels, earned for him a fellowship in the American Association for the Advancement of Science and also a biographical citation in American Men of Science. During the "anti-evolution craze" of the 1920's, Professor Utterback was strangely obsessed with the theoretical feasibility of reconciling science and the Scriptures; and in his oft-repeated lecture, "The Great Life Cycle," he argued that both special creation and evolution were entirely possible. Utterback's theories received a modicum of national recognition and support when Dr. Walter Hough, the Curator of the Smithsonian Institution, declared that "Utterback's correlation of science and the gospel is the best that has yet appeared."[18]

Elsewhere Moffat took another dig at Utterback:

> William I. Utterback of the Biology Department, in his oft-repeated lecture, "The Second Triangle," had made a determined effort to enlighten the laity and to reconcile the theory of evolution with the Scriptures. It is conceivable, however, that Utterback even further confused many of his auditors.[19]

So what was this theory that earned the praise of the Smithsonian's Walter Hough and the disdain of Marshall's Charles Moffat? The archives has a copy of an Utterback treatise in pamphlet form, signed "Compliments of the author to Marshall College Library. Dec. 4, 1928," the essay's full title being, "The Great Life Cycle: A Conception of the Past, Present and Future as Presented in Cyclic Form from Fire to Fire on Basis of Science and Scripture." In it, he

- says the Bible is "infallible," for "surely, an All-wise Providence would not permit errors to be handed down in His Word"

- identifies with those who "are neither extreme fundamentalists, nor radical liberalists"

- claims that the days of creation in Genesis 1 correspond to geologic eras—the Day/Age theory, the Third Day being Paleozoic, the Fourth, Mesozoic

- says that the "results of preaching the gospel and the extension of the church all over the world" are "the greatest evidences of the coming of that Perfect Day, the wonderful epoch of supernaturalism," when "the wolf and the lamb shall feed together" and "a little child shall lead them" and when also "the saints possess the kingdom" as "priests of God and Christ"

- speaks without irony or apology of Noah's flood as "the result of . . . divine punishment," of the end-times' "lake of fire" that awaits unbelievers, and of the reality of "Satan"

(In a side note, *The Parthenon* reported that the college was happy to schedule, as part of the artists series, James Breasted, head of the University of Chicago's Oriental Institute, who delivered a thoroughly Darwinian account of the emergence of man.)

(Darwin Update)

Of course, feelings still run high over Darwinism, though there have been many developments in the disputes surrounding it throughout the intervening years (nearly a century since the Scopes trial). Evolutionary theory has achieved dominance in academia (major research universities, such as the Ivy Leagues), prominent museums (such as the Smithsonian and Chicago's Field Museum), the mainstream media (e.g., *National Geographic* and the legacy networks), and government publications and displays (such as one finds in the National Park Service's visitors center at the Grand Canyon and Dinosaur Monument). Still, there has been lively dissent, with parties to the debate holding credentials one might not anticipate, given Professor Selvage's take on the matter.

Richard Dawkins has continued the tradition of contempt for anyone who would gainsay evolutionary theory. Less strident was Harvard's Stephen Jay Gould, who tweaked the story so as to accommodate the "Cambrian explosion," positing "punctuated equilibrium." He also supplied an expression reflecting the predominant 1920s faculty position at Marshall—NOMA (Non-Overlapping Magisteria), leaving science and religion to enjoy their supposedly non-conflicting realms of authority.

Another approach has found its way through the courts, the idea of "intelligent design," without specific reference to the biblical creation account. At this point, it's a non-starter in the public schools since, in the Dover case, the judge ruled that requiring teachers to note it as an option simply provided a wedge for the traditional biblical account to find its way into the curriculum (thus an affront to both church-state separation and science itself). The presiding judge opined that no statement that referred to God (the intelligent designer) was scientifically valid, but distinguished philosopher, Alvin Plantinga, threw out a counter-example: The sentence, "God has caused nine-foot tall rabbits to populate the streets of Cleveland" both refers to God and is scientifically falsifiable. Of course, this didn't change things legally, but it did show how some powerful officials can get out over their intellectual skis in pontificating.

It turns out that some secularists have started having doubts about the Darwinian account, including Jerry Fodor of MIT, CUNY, and Rutgers (a philosopher of the cognitive sciences, with a PhD from Princeton, who wrote *What Darwin Got Wrong* [Farrar, Straus, and Giroux]), and Thomas Nagel, a Harvard trained philosopher who, in *Mind and Cosmos: Why the Materialist Neo-Darwinian Conception of Nature is Almost Certainly False* (Oxford), argued that consciousness could not arise purely from matter.

Then there were the Christian philosophers and scientists who argued, against Darwin, that intelligent design was more plausible. The group includes Catholic biochemist Michael Behe (PhD, Pennsylvania), who advanced the notion of "irreducible complexity" in *Darwin's Black Box* (Free Press); Presbyterian legal scholar, Phillip Johnson (JD, Chicago), whose *Darwin on Trial* (Regnery) and *Defeating Darwinism by Opening Minds* (InterVarsity) argued against slavish commitment to "methodological naturalism," which arbitrarily excluded all reference to the supernatural; and Baptist William Dembski (PhD's in mathematics and philosophy, respectively from Chicago and Illinois-Chicago), who has worked with probabilities, as in *The Design Inference* (Cambridge).

The case against Darwinism continues on a variety of fronts, including insistence on the difference between items which are clearly verifiable or falsifiable (Bernoulli's Principle; Ohm's Law) and cosmological and historical theories, which are not so since they are one-off, non-repeatable, vastly-distant events (the Big Bang; the origin of species through natural selection). And a particularly troublesome set of phenomena for the Darwinists arise in the aesthetic realm. How does "survival of the fittest" produce appreciation for beauty when some of the most pleasingly arresting views on earth are to be had in some of the most deadly places to be found (e.g., Wadi Rum; the Himalayas). The empirical practice of "inference to the best explanation"/"abduction" is not obviously the evolutionist's best friend in these situations.

Of course, among Christians, there is a range of takes on how or whether evolution and old-earth geology are compatible with the biblical account, just as there were in the 1920s at Marshall. Some have chosen to be "theistic evolutionists" (with God's using natural selection to effect the emergence of biological kingdoms, phyla, classes, orders, families, etc.); others, "old-earth special creationists" (with God's putting a soul into an animal at a certain stage of historical development); and yet others "young-earth special creationists" (with the world's being fewer than ten thousand years old, and Adam's being a special creation of God, along with horses, fish, and birds). This latter view is argued and demonstrated through the Ark Encounter (a display-filled, full-scale replica of Noah's Ark, about a three-hour drive west of Marshall).

All of this comes in the context of Thomas Kuhn's seminal work, *The Structure of Scientific Revolutions* (Chicago, 1962), which introduced the notion of overarching "paradigms" or models, through which "ordinary science" is conducted; which are secured by a combination of rational and irrational commitments; which are subject to overthrow when "anomalies" or difficulties mount up and the theory's champions die off; and which may be supplanted by alternative paradigms with their own programs of "ordinary science." Also impactful was Karl Popper's *The Logic of Scientific Discovery* (Julius Springer, Hutchinson & Co., 1934; Routledge, 2005). It laid waste to the notion that a sweeping theory could be finally and smugly verified. On this model, its validity rests upon its being genuinely up for grabs pending subsequent experience, a posture antithetical to the conceit that "untouchable" is a scientific desideratum.

"Progress, Retrogression, or What?"

Evolution wasn't the only modern development on students' minds, as the words of this March 8, 1928 editorial note ("Progress, Retrogression, or What?"):

> Not long ago we heard an eloquent sermon on "The Downward Trend of Modern Civilization." The old sky pilot, a godly and

righteous man, who was no doubt doing and preaching according to his lights, was tirading [sic] and berating society for its wickedness. He especially bemoaned the fact that the present-day flapper at 18 knew more about the sex problem than grandmothers did a generation ago.

Modern society is undeniably gross and materialistic and far from perfect, but we do not consider the flappers' knowledge of the sex problem an indication of the world's "going to the devil," as the good man expressed it. Furthermore, we consider the squeamish and shamefaced reluctance of many parents to recognize and deal frankly with the facts and problems of sex as an ignorant attitude that ought to be abandoned. Such an attitude of mind that looks upon sexual impulses as fundamentally evil and as a sign of man's degradation is clearly of medieval origin. We are encouraged to know that such an attitude appears to be decreasing among the better educated of the younger generation.

From such a modern standpoint, one column looked back five decades, the headline proclaiming:

Times Ain't What They Used to Be.
Feature Editor Digs Up Rules of 1872
Room Rent Free in the Good Old Days and Board $2.75 per Week
Demerits Given for Talking and Whispering in Class or in the Halls
[one demerit for each offense]

The article explained that thirty demerits meant "admonishment before the whole school"; that excuses should not include "not hearing the bell, not being able to prepare the lesson, being out late the preceding night, writing letters, and mislaying books or articles of apparel"; furthermore, "No student shall enter class drunk or under the influence of intoxicating liquors."

One gets the strong sense that "liberation" was the golden idea in that day. Listen as December 27, 1924 *Parthenon* exults over a chapel address, in an article, "Lo! A Scholar Speaks":

Rabbi Feinstein's address to the college student body two weeks ago ranks high among the relatively few scholarly talks that are given from our chapel rostrum. Rarely are our mental appetites so satisfied in chapel services with such choice morsels of food for thought.

To say that the rabbi's address was a remarkable one would be putting it mildly. It was a classic. Fearlessly expressing with forceful diction and clarifying logic the modern scholar's open-minded scientific attitude toward education, the speaker gained from us our lasting admiration.

The only regrettable feature of the address was his statement to the fact that it was the first time he'd ever had the opportunity to talk to such an audience on such a topic. His message ought to be heard in every college throughout the country and the truth therein embodied ought to become the watchword of everyone who has the daring to call himself educated.

We highly congratulate Rabbi Feinstein on his splendid address and also the chapel program committee on their securing such a speaker. In the future we would be pleased to have a more generous sprinkling of addresses of the nature of Rabbi Feinstein's and few less expositions on medieval metaphysics.

It's not clear what was meant by "medieval metaphysics" (Thomas Aquinas's appropriation of Aristotle's "teleological cause"; Maimonides's *via negativa*?; Anselm's ontological argument or Gaunilo's retort?). Maybe it was just his way to dismiss the other speakers as old fashioned. Be that as it may, we do get a taste of medieval (or First Century or contemporary) metaphysics on the same page—"Thoughts Concerning Christmas" by E. Turner Stump. It's not without its curious observations on ethics, but there's enough of the traditional in it to stir whatever medieval hearts might be on campus:

> The first Christmas was the culmination, though few recognized it as such, of the Messianic hope of the Hebrew people. The coming of this day had been the burden of their song and prophecy and had been anticipated in their forms of worship for countless years. It was only fitting that the first Christmas should be ushered in by a special song more beautiful than any songs of the antiphonal choirs and nobler in thought than the strains of Moses and David. It was fitting that the expectant and symbolic worship of earth should be augmented now by the worship of heaven. And so it was, for angels sang the message, "Peace on earth to men of good will." It is also well to remember that kings and common-folk united in a joyous hope although vague. We have a right to say therefore that hopefulness was the outstanding feature of the first Christmas.
>
> After the centuries have lapsed we come once more to Christmas time. We look about us and at first we are depressed. We say that the hope of the first Christmas was unwarranted and that the angel song has proved meaningless. This is quite natural on hasty and superficial thought, especially in a day when shadows

cast by the great war still linger on the earth. But on more careful thought our feeling of depression must pass away. Today there is more earnest effort and more sincere thought on the problem of making the angel song true than ever before in human history. Today the ethical system of yesterday, incomplete, incompatible with each other and depending on the dictum of a dead leader, such as Confucius, or Mohammed, have become unified, and codified, if you please, and centered around the person of a living leader who is a rallying force for the glorious moral achievements of the future. This leader is called "Jesus." He was born on Christmas day. It would be possible to dwell at length on the countless blessings of today made possible by the coming of this man "Jesus." It is not too broad an assertion to say that all the great hope for the future that the world has is because of Him.

Sayre's Rants Against "Pie-Faced" Deplorables

Continuing the theme of social struggle (with Wallace Sayre speaking as editor-in-chief of *The Parthenon*), we read "Why Do We Mourn?":

> There is abroad in the land a current feeling among altogether too many people that the liberal arts colleges of America are hotbeds of radicalism and atheism, feeding their students on crass materialistic philosophies and robbing them of their faith in the religion that they were taught at their mother's knee. Of late we have heard so many people mouth over this mournful formula that we feel constrained to say a word in behalf of the educational system which, we feel, has given us a wider view and higher conception of the life it is accused of debasing. Strange to say those who most strongly condemn the liberal arts colleges are usually those who have never attended one. All of which gives them more authority to speak with power and unction. It is one of the tragedies of present-day civilization that those people who have the fewest ideas are usually those persons who shout them most vociferously. Narrowminded orthodoxy has always been the Bourbon of thought; it learns nothing, neither can it forget.
>
> The modern-day liberal arts college is asking its incoming students nothing more nor nothing less than the question Elijah asked back in the dawn of Judea—"Choose ye whom you will serve, God or Baal." And the average college student who is usually prayed for because of his "forgetting his mother's religion" is usually doing nothing more than seriously asking himself

whether he can be satisfied with the Baal of authority and with all the good things his worshipers are promised in this world and the next. Mistaken zealots may mourn when a bright youth suddenly bursts the bonds of the mental slavery of authority, but there is more rejoicing in the realms of eternal truth over such a lad than ninety and nine who continue to do the goose step and become moneyed successes.

A human being becomes a man the moment he begins to question the things he believes and it becomes an individual the moment he dares to overthrow authority as such and think for himself...

This same Editor-in-Chief Wallace Sayre seemed to know no limits in defaming those who would disagree with him. In November 1938, he rails against what he calls "Pie-Faced Reverence" ("pie-faced" being a synonym for "vacuous" or "stupid"):

There are a great many people in the country who sincerely feel that some principles, beliefs, and institutions should be above all criticism, and that it is disloyal and sacrilegious, or at the least an exhibition of impropriety, to discuss them in any other spirit than that of unquestioning reverence. These people's sensitive propensity to be "shocked" leads them to avoid all discussions which may bring out differences of personal opinion and sentiment on fundamental questions of politics and economics, and especially of religion. Of course the attitude of mind which produces this conspiracy of silence is based on sheer stupidity which makes it all the harder to deal with successfully.

This attitude of mind of which we speak is the identical type of mind possessed by those who crucified Christ and those holy ones who excommunicated and burned at the stake the reformers of the middle ages amid the mental applause of all the righteous minded. Today this type of mind due to necessitous conditions has changed its means to attain the desired end. Unable to no longer [sic] successfully excommunicate or burn at the stake (except with hooded robes on) this type of mind maintains itself in power and influence by keeping those who differ from the accepted out of jobs. Just recently, we read in one of the state's leading religious periodicals a Sunday school lesson written by a self-confessed disciple of the Great Teacher, who taught the world to love their enemies and return good for evil, urging the educational authorities of the state to kick out, bag and baggage, those college professors "with their pockets filled with diplomas and their heads full of sawdust" who had the daring to question the finality of a single teaching of the apostle Paul . . ."

Then in another effusion of purple prose (May 4, 1936), Sayre took on the library's decision to remove certain periodicals from display:

> The Parthenon wonders if the removal of "too liberal" magazines from the college library is to become an adopted policy at Marshall. The recent removal of the New Republic, preceded by a similar removal of the American Mercury, seems to point in just that direction. This policy of benevolent protection has, beyond a doubt, its advantages. It is safe and—we almost said sane. It brings adulation from those who bask pleasantly in the light of yesterdays, in things that "were good for our fathers and are good enough for me." The status quo is always popular with taxpayers, unless it is a return to "the good old days" that is more popular. And pious worshipers of things as they are sigh with satisfaction at such thoughtful regulation of the intellectual pursuits of wild-eyed college students.
>
> But what of the student? He has been laboring under the delusion that there is merit in knowing both sides of a case before he draws conclusions. He has taken too literally the command of one who said "Seek the truth and the truth shall make you free." Somehow his teachers have failed to tell him that all the truth has been discovered and that further search is heresy and impertinence. And here he is in college, possessed with a laudable desire for the facts of life and society, but ignorant of the fact that it is already discovered and stored away in the present institutions of society and possessed by all the believers in the status quo. He does not know that The American Magazine contains the truth attractively set forth in the life-stories of altruistic captains of industry, while The New Republic and The American Mercury, and their like, are a fraud, snare and delusion, the creation of the devil, the evil invention of wild-eyed fanatics, old bolsheviks, and radicals, to lead astray the young and gullible and defenseless college student who is all the more an easy prey because he imagines he has a rational mind.
>
> So the college student must learn to humbly walk in the paths of his fathers—nor dare to brazenly think on things which puzzle him. He must learn that he owes all to present institutions of society, nor dare to be dissatisfied with what he is. He must throw away his hammer and blow always and mightily upon his horn—And the utopia of endless mediocrity will be with us forever and ever. Amen.

Incidentally, Sayre went on to teach political science at Columbia University and his tart tongue was evident in the 1950s, when he was credited with what's become known as "Sayre's Law"—"The politics of the university are so intense because the stakes are so low."

The Birth of a Nation

Fitting the times, the *Parthenon* editorialized against the Ku Klux Klan, faulting *The Birth of a Nation*, which was screened appreciatively in President Woodrow Wilson's White House. Surprisingly, though, the paper ventured to grant that the KKK might have had its place in the beginning, but insisted that it had never been laudable.

> With the assertion that this nation was, as a nation, in reality born in the struggle of the Civil War we have no immediate quarrel, but that a hooded organization, relying wholly on the fears and superstitions of an ignorant race but recently freed from the degrading state of slavery—that such an organization had any beneficial effect and the creation of a nation we do [not] deny. However necessary such an organization may have been at that time, due to the lust for power on the part of a group of the conquerors, it has no permanent place in a government based on the promise that all government should exist for the benefit of the governed.
>
> A contemporary organization, similar in most respects to the hooded clans of the sixties, with a more exclusive ban on those whom they deemed [less than] "one hundred per cent, Americans," is basing its explanation for existence on an emotional appeal to a misplaced nationalism, racial prejudice, and a perverted interpretation of historical incidents. That this organization in its original form had a necessary function to perform is perhaps true, but with a fault inherent in all institutions it failed to realize when its purpose had been accomplished. It lost sight of the end in view. It has set out to "free the White South from the heel of the Black South, and in its fanaticism tried to crush the Black South under the heel of the White South." Today the exponents of this particular brand of Americanism would have us believe that their organization was a potential power in the creating of our nation. Do they lose sight of the fact that their own leaders came to realize that an organization founded on secrecy and relying on force and superstition was a menace to popular government and immediately dissolved the organization they had created?

That public opinion is still a conglomeration of emotional recreations savored with a minimum of rational observations is best illustrated by the popularity of a picture filmed several years ago and possessing all the relative imperfections of the screen at that time with its crude scenes and poor acting. This picture enjoys a great popularity because it appeals to and feeds on ignorant racial hatred while at the same time affording the applauder a not inconsiderable emotional self-pride.

A nation basing its existence on popular government lives up to its name only when it promotes the welfare of its people, and through them, the welfare of humanity. No organization denying to certain groups of a nation the privileges granted to other members of the same nation can claim to have a rightful place in the life of that nation.

Booze and Fashion

The era of the flapper and bathtub gin touched but didn't much shape Marshall. President Morris Shawkey (1923–1935) was center stage in the school's response. For one thing, he was a keen supporter of prohibition (of beverage alcohol)—the "Noble Experiment." His stance likely resonated with the majority of the student body, and many of them, both students and faculty, petitioned President Herbert Hoover to enforce the Eighteenth Amendment. When the Twenty-First Amendment repealed prohibition, Shawkey predicted that it would be reinstated with some modifications.[20]

When a number of girls attending summer school wore shorts to class, a scandalous photo of the crew appeared around the world, and Shawkey caught heat for this display of immodesty. But he stood his ground, assuring critics that "the girls are from good homes and are of fine character and good habits" and "to know them is to respect them very highly." To one who gainsaid the moral tone of the campus, he responded, "I think moral conditions . . . at Marshall College are as good as are found in the best of colleges . . . I think all of our faculty are church members . . . Marshall College students are as high minded and honest as would be found anywhere." Be that as it may, one professor observed that things could get dicey at the regular dances held on and off campus, due to the influx of "so many rough boys from the coal mines" who came in to dance with the coeds, with fights breaking out regularly.[21]

4

Depression and War

BEFORE 1957, MARSHALL STUDENTS were required to note their religious preference on application and registration forms, and in 1935, a summary showed that, of 1,950 students, only 14 percent had no particular affiliation, with none self-designating as atheist. And, for the first time, they found a Unitarian. In those days, the vast majority were Methodist, Baptist, and Presbyterian, with a fair representation of Catholics. By 1940, nearly a hundred Catholics had joined the Newman Club, and a B'nai B'rith Hillel chapter was in place for the handful of Jews on campus. Sizing up the mix, Marshall historian Charles Moffat observed, "In a real sense the Appalachian region was typical of the American 'Bible Belt' in that the mountain people were fundamentalist sectarians," the effect being, "In general, it can be said that most Marshall College students appeared somewhat naive when they attempted to discuss—much less argue—theological or philosophical tenets with the more sophisticated students from the Northeastern states."[22]

The Centennial Celebration

In 1937, the school celebrated "One Hundred Years of Marshall College,"[23] an event featuring the following:

- a May 13, Sunday-morning baccalaureate service in Keith-Albee theater, including invocation, sermon, and benediction by, respectively, Reverends Peirce, Speer, and Mauze; special and congregational music including "O Lord Send The Fire," "All Hail the Power," "Shepherd of Israel," and "Beautiful Saviour"

40

- the printed text of Reverend Speer's sermon (he having "for many years . . . commanded the missionary forces of the so-called northern branch of the great Presbyterian Church"), a sermon that traced the biblical theme of "building up" (as opposed to tearing down), as illustrated in the epistles, by the biblical patriarchs, in the works of Pericles and Michelangelo, and in the work of English writers, Lytton Strachey (negatively) and William Blake (positively)

- the printed text of the commencement address ("Is Moderation Dead?"), delivered by Douglas Southall Freedman, editor of the Richmond *News Leader*, a message in which he celebrated "the old, evangelical spirit that made the 1830's one of the greatest decades in American education," an era that saw the progression from the Sunday School, where children were taught to read in order that they might enjoy the "sweets of the gospel" to the "establishment of the colleges where religious influence might give form, color, and perspective to a new picture of American life"

- the observation that the College of Arts and Science then included the departments of political science, philosophy, sociology, Bible, journalism, dramatic art, speech, mechanical drawing and physical education

- the texts of prayers, one referencing [quoting James 1:17] "the Father of Lights, in whom is no variableness, neither shadow of turning" (A. B. Leamer, pastor of St. Paul's Lutheran Church) and another speaking of "the God of our fathers and our God" (B. P. Taylor, pastor of Johnson Memorial Methodist Church)

Spiritual and Moral Concerns

In these years, the college was intent upon securing and advancing the spiritual and moral welfare of the student body as well as maintaining spiritual presence in the community. Here are items from the 1930s (mainly from *The Parthenon*) which reflect those concerns. They occurred under the presidencies of Morris Shawkey (1923–1935) and James Allen (1935–1942):

- John R. Sampey, the president of Southern Baptist Theological Seminary in Louisville delivered the 1938 baccalaureate message ("A Challenge to the Great Adventure"), with invocation by Ward

Harvey of First Methodist Episcopal Church and benediction by Byron Wilkinson of Fifth Avenue Baptist Church. The seniors assembled at First Presbyterian Church for a five-minute processional to the Keith Albee Theater.

- President Shawkey was the November 18, 1931, speaker at the Huntington Ministerial Association meeting at First Methodist Episcopal Church, Rev. W. H. Hooper of Highlawn Presbyterian presiding; in May of 1932, Shawkey also spoke at the Guyandotte Association meeting of the Baptist Young People's Union.

- The 1930–1931 catalogue declares, "The great majority of the students enrolling here are young men and women of fine character and habits and the college is under obligation to protect them from the damaging influences of moral or intellectual profligates."

- The week of February 8, 1938, Episcopal rector, E. E. Mowers, brought a devotional message in chapel; in March of that same year, Rabbi Maurice Goldblatt of Roanoke spoke to the same group on "Democracy Today."

- Rev. Jesse Pindell Peirce of the Congregational Church spoke to the International Relations Club in February, 1938 on "The Mad Race for Armaments," in which he concluded, "We are building a Frankenstein that will some day destroy us"; in May, he returned to the club to speak on "Americanism," saying that it wasn't "worship of state, widespread 'patriotic' propaganda and jingoism, the Daughters of the American Revolution, the American Legion and other similar organizations"; he decried compulsory military training at state schools, the ejection of socialist candidate Norman Thomas from New Jersey, and the arrest of conscientious objectors.

- In January of 1938, West Virginia University history professor Oliver P. Chitwood spoke at a Marshall assembly celebrating Robert E. Lee's 131st birthday. Chitwood said that "simplicity and spirituality" were his greatest characteristics.

- In a February, 1938 assembly of seniors, President Allen delivered a message ("On the Way Out"), closing with "You are truly God's chosen among the young people of your community. You should be proud you are college students but at the same time careful to justify that pride."

- In February, 1938, the Huntington chapter of the National Council of Jews and Christians (of which U.S. Supreme Court chief justice Charles Evans Hughes was a founder), scheduled an interfaith program in the city auditorium. While in Huntington, they also spoke to students at Marshall, the panelists being Rev. Gottschall of the First Christian Church of Baltimore, Father Stephens of the Richmond Diocese, and Rabbi Lieberman of the Madison Street Temple in Baltimore.

- The February 10, 1932 *Parthenon* reports, "Gypsy Smith, Jr., famed nomadic evangelist spoke this morning in assembly. Mr. Smith, who is holding a series of meetings in the First Presbyterian Church, is the son of internationally known minister, Gypsy Smith, who was chosen in 1913 by Lloyd George, prime minister of England, as the first Christian worker to enter the trenches. Mr. Smith mentioned the work of his father and applied Christian living to college life."

- The November 15, 1933, *Parthenon* reported a drop in the total number of stated religious preferences within the student body, with the largest denominational representatives—Methodist and Baptist—dropping seventy-seven (from four hundred twenty-two) and eighty-three respectively. Presbyterians went from two hundred seventy-eight to two hundred twenty-one. The "nones" rose from one hundred seventy-one to two hundred four; the Church of Christ lost thirty-one; the Roman Catholics dropped from one hundred three to eighty-seven ; other losses were recorded (from largest to smallest group) by Episcopal, Lutheran, Protestant, Congregational, Christian Science, Church of God, Seventh Day Adventist, Missionary Holiness, and Latter Day Saints. United Brethren grew from twelve to thirteen, Orthodox from one to two. Four groups hitherto unlisted appeared in the count—Nazarenes, United Baptist, Evangelical, and Salvation Army.

- The December 18th, 1934, issue of *The Parthenon* pictured six men who are "members of the recently formed Marshall Ministerial Association." In March of 1935, they held an assembly featuring Father Norton of St. Joseph's Catholic Church, Rabbi Soskin of Ohev Sholem Temple, and J.W. Yoho of Madison Avenue Church of Christ. That same month, they announced a series of devotionals to be given "during vacant assembly periods or the lunch hour of all Wednesdays during which there is an assembly." Still, in the 1930 yearbook, where graduates were listed according to their leading associations, we find

Y affiliation listed as prominently as "Greek" membership. In that issue, group and roster pages list twenty-four in the YMCA and three hundred in the YWCA.

- In December, 1934, art professor Emmett Myers named his favorite Christmas paintings, beginning with Raphael's *Sistine Madonna*, and extending to Correggio's *Holy Night* and *Adoration of the Magi* as well as Murillo's *Adoration of the Shepherds*: "Something heavenly hovers about each one, a suggestion of world peace and hope and the spirit which has come to mean Christmas."

- An ad by The Tog Shop had spiritual and moral overtones, saying, "The consciousness of good clothes is, in and of itself, a source of moral strength, second only to that of a clean conscience." They proudly sold "John Wanamaker's Old Line Tailoring," connecting them to the legacy of the Philadelphia merchant (and later U.S. Postmaster General) who was an outspoken patron of evangelical causes.

- The Christian Alliance (*Parthenon*, Feb. 4, 1938) served as the college's interdenominational association of Christian students. One of their sponsored presentations was a Seminar in Radiant Christian Living, with lectures by Mrs. Jessie Burrall Eubank in the library building's art museum. Topics included "Unexplored Resources in the Personality," "Spiritual Power for Daily Use," "Dating and Mating," and "Acquaintance, Friendship, Courtship, Marriage, What?"

Hmmm

The January 18, 1933 *Parthenon* featured a photo from the University of Kansas of three students "considered the most appropriately garbed" for the annual "Hobo Day." Though this was not considered transgressive in the day, and kids would dress that way on Halloween, it would not likely pass muster today, in that it would be seen to demean the "homeless."

The March 6, 1935, Parthenon announced a repeat performance of Anatole France's, *The Man Who Married a Dumb Wife*.

The War Years

At the beginning of WWII, Marshall had over two thousand students, but by 1944, enrollment had dropped to seven hundred twenty, as many of her men went off to war. (The 1945 yearbook names five "that will not return" as well as one hundred fifty who would have graduated that year had they not served in the conflict.) Intercollegiate athletics was suspended, as was building construction and maintenance. Though the school hosted sixteen hundred men for the Army Air Corps and Naval Reserve Air Cadet Training programs, they were not actual students of the college.[24]

The April 5, 1938 *Parthenon* reported the results of a poll initiated at the national level by Brown University, with particular focus on the Marshall results, tapping into four hundred eighty-eight students. It revealed that 4 percent would refuse to fight in any war; that 19 percent would fight for the sake of American interests abroad; and that 66 percent would take up arms only if the nation faced invasion. The poll also assessed sentiment regarding Japan's aggression in the Far East, including the "Rape of Nanking," which had occurred earlier that year. Responses varied, from boycott, to withdrawal of US troops from the region, to severance of relations. Of course, the Munich Accords and Hitler's invasion of the Sudetenland would not occur until that fall. Dunkirk and the Battle of Britain were still two years away, the bombing of Pearl Harbor over three years away. So much was yet to unfold, but this was the mood on campus in the spring of 1938. (The March 15, 1935, issue reported that the "Marshall Peace League" had the backing of the "majority of campus leaders," a group that included the presidents of several sororities and fraternities, the home economics club, the women's athletic association, and the YMCA.

Among the post-war students were a number injured in the conflict. They formed a Disabled American Veterans group on campus, with Robert Britton as faculty advisor and Rev. Hanley Pinson as chaplain. Their focus was "the care of its sick members and aid for the widows and orphans of fallen comrades." Eighteen are pictured in the 1947 yearbook.

Though not himself a Marshall graduate, John Grove Barker, the school's tenth president (1971–1974) served as an army rifleman in the Philippines during World War II, earning the Combat Infantry Badge and a Bronze Star. His successor, Robert Bruce Hayes (1974–1983), also saw service in that war, he as a Marine. Sam Edward Clagg, Hayes's successor as interim president in 1984, served as a Marine officer in the South Pacific and China (1943–1946).[25]

In a 1999 interview, Clagg got emotional when recalling his time at war, where he saw combat in the bloody battles of Peleliu and Okinawa: "If a break had gone against us here and there, we could be speaking German or Japanese. It was that close." He continued, "I don't want to glorify the war. It was horrible, but it helped us get out of the Depression. Huntington really took off during the 1940s. All the plants here were booming, and Marshall really took off after the war when all the boys came home from the war . . . These were the best of times, and the worst of times." He added, "Thank God for the G.I. Bill. A lot of servicemen would have been on the streets without jobs if it hadn't been for the G.I. Bill. It gave them an opportunity to go to college. Marshall got some really seasoned students after the war."[26]

Of course, the war impacted Marshall-connected people on the home front as well. Estelle Belanger, a 1935 graduate, was working in Washington, D.C. as a file clerk for the Civil Service Administration when war broke out. Back in Huntington, the *Herald-Advertiser* had lost one her reporters, Ned Brown, to military service, and the editor asked her to take his place on the condition that she relinquish the job to Brown should he return and want it back. He did, in fact, make it through the war, but he ended up opening a radio station in Florida in 1946, so she remained at the paper. As she recalls, the churches were full—"They say there are no atheists in foxholes. There weren't any at home either." (Incidentally, her brother was a priest and her two sisters were nuns.)[27]

5

Post-War

THE LATE 1940S AND the 1950s are often viewed as halcyon days, a time when "baby boomers" appeared in families newly blessed by peace and prosperity. Billy Graham's crusades in Los Angeles (1949) and New York (1957) were stunning events. In Los Angeles, with eight weeks of preaching in a huge tent, Graham saw three hundred fifty thousand attend, with three thousand making decisions for Christ. In New York's Madison Square Garden, five hundred seventy-five thousand attended in the first month alone, with eighteen thousand five hundred professing new trust in Jesus as Savior and Lord.

Television families were wholesome (*Ozzie and Harriett*; *Father Knows Best*; *Leave It To Beaver*; *Make Room for Daddy*); good-guy/bad-guy Westerns were plentiful (*Gunsmoke*; *Rifleman*; *Lone Ranger*; *Bonanza*); those pursuing criminal justice were admirable (*Dragnet*; *Peter Gunn*; *Superman*; *Perry Mason*); the cartoons were fun (*Road Runner*; *Mighty Mouse*; *Woody Woodpecker*; anything Disney); the comedy clean (*Jack Benny*; *You Bet Your Life*; *Milton Berle*; *Red Skelton*); and the adult "babysitters" were trustworthy (Captain Kangaroo; Buffalo Bob Smith on *Howdy Doody*; Sherri Lewis with Lambchop).

Of course, not everything was rosy in the 1950s and early 1960s. Jim Crow racial laws and customs were still in effect, with the March on Selma pending. Allen Ginsberg's 1955 poem, "Howl," and Jack Kerouac's 1957 journal, *On the Road*, helped launch the Beat Generation, with its counter-culture disaffection and interest in drugs. The threat of nuclear attack from the Soviet Union led school officials to outfit kids with dog tags and families to build fallout shelters. Still, there was something of a national consensus across a range of ethnicities and economic strata that traditional values were there for a good reason, including their biblical underpinnings.

Lander Beal and the SCA

Lander Beal, who served as campus pastor in the 1950s, was a major spiritual presence on campus. Esteemed trustworthy by the college and pastors of the region, he was able and motivated to enlarge the Christian witness on campus. He lived well up into his eighties, and this selection from his obituary provides a quick look at the arc of his life:

> Lander completed graduate and post-graduate studies at High Point College, Brevard College, Duke University, Emory University and Methodist Theological School in Ohio. He was a retired minister of the United Methodist Church. He served as campus pastor at Marshall University and helped coordinate the work of nine denominations to build the Campus Christian Center. The family asked that memorial gifts be sent to either First Methodist in Huntington or the Campus Christian Center.

In those days, he oversaw the Student Christian Association (SCA), providing an "opportunity to experience ecumenicity," not meant as a separate group, but as a coalition of existing ministries. As such, it gained support from a range of sources, including local churches (e.g., St. Paul's Lutheran and Fifth Avenue Baptist) as well as the West Virginia offices of the American Baptists, Christian Church, Episcopal Diocese, Presbyterian Synod, and the Methodists.[28] SCA was established on campus in 1952 by Yale Divinity School graduate, Rev. John E. Surgener, whom Marshall supplied an office, a telephone, and some supplies. A year later, Surgener took a church in New England, and Lander Beale succeeded him. According to Beale, the SCA existed

> ... to proclaim the Gospel of Jesus Christ in the academic community ... Our mission is to present the truth of the Christian faith amid the conflicting viewpoints on campus, to witness to the redeeming words of Jesus Christ, and to help students, faculty, and administration to recognize their responsibility under God.

He added:

> Part of our program is training Christian laymen, i.e., one who has accepted the Christian faith and has agreed to support the Church

with his prayers, his time, and his money. More opportunity must be given to the Campus Community. Giving is a part of worship. Improvement here can help our program but it doesn't fulfill the total program.

We must never forget that our purpose is to meet the religious needs of the College Community and we as members can help meet these needs only when we have given, and continue to give, our whole selves to God. It is then that we have something of value to share, the love of God for men.

SCA held a seminar in April on the topic, "Do you believe college drinking is a moral issue?" and *The Campus Chimes* printed some of the responses: The dean of men, Harrold Willey, said the student leaders were doing a good job controlling things—case in point the Military Ball in March; Sally Montgomery, Alpha Chi Omega president, urged moderation and observed, "I have found that I can have a good time without drinking"; Leo Imperi of the music department took exception to "functions whose sole purpose is drinking" and said, "If college students have never drunk at home, it is unwise for them to start under the guidance of companions"; Mary Marshall, chaplain at the freshman dorm said,

> I don't believe drinking of any sort has a place on campus because of its potential of leading to other issues. It is a problem because so much is done in social organizations. College students are old enough to realize the physical dangers of alcoholism. Actually, it takes more courage to refuse to drink than to indulge.

Before Thanksgiving, SCA sponsored a service, one for which ROTC drill was suspended to allow attendance by the cadets. Looking forward to Christmas, they also scheduled a play, *Star Song*, a "dramatization of the night Jesus was born," and a program at "the State Mental Hospital in Barboursville." This in addition to a daunting range and depth of regular activities reported in their 1956–1957 summary, from which we learn they had two hundred twenty-five members variously involved in thirty-one Thursday night meetings, forty worship services, four visits to the "Colored Children Home," weekly vespers in four dorms, and fifteen "firesides." Three hundred sixty students came to the office for counseling, and Beal himself prayed at four sporting events, engaged in sports with students eighteen times, attended forty SCA planning meetings, and preached twenty sermons. And this is just a sampling.

The Student Christian Association (SCA) took a new name in the fall of 1959, becoming the Campus Christian Fellowship (CCW), "to make it a more inclusive rather than exclusive organization where all members of the campus are welcome." As Beal put it, membership "would be made up of each student that is a member of the Church. Therefore, each church member is a member of this Fellowship. Our task is getting each member envolved [sic] in the Campus ministry. As you can see, this would not be another organization, but 'the church at work on the campus.' "

Beal was well regarded at Marshall, with glowing words sent his way in the yearbook: "So that our religious values will not be lost in the hubbub of school activities," he, "with a broad smile and cheerful word for everyone has helpful advice and words of encouragement which are welcomed by all students who consult with him" (1955); "No matter how pressing the problem or how busy he is, he can always smile or give a friendly wink, and reflect his Christian view of life" (1957).

The Campus Chimes

In the winter of 1959, and under Lander Beal's supervision, a new publication, *The Campus Chimes*, came on the scene, the same year construction began on the new Campus Christian Center. Elizabeth Older was editor, and the articles were respectful of prominent evangelical figures of the 1950s, noting, for instance, a campus visit by Frank Laubach, whose "Each One Teach One Literacy Movement" had extended to ninety-one countries over the thirty years of his ministry. (He developed the program as a Congregationalist missionary among Muslims in a remote part of the Philippines.) Laubach was quoted to say, "Regular armies are not what those people need; they need an 'army of compassion' to win their love. If we don't send out this army we will lose the world to the Communists." (Incidentally, he's the only missionary every to be honored on a U.S. postage stamp.)

That spring, they also ran an interview with Don Moomaw, pastor of First Presbyterian Church in Berkeley, California. In Huntington, he was the youth night speaker at a citywide "preaching mission." Moomaw was a two-time All-American lineman at UCLA, later inducted into the College Football Hall of Fame. Drafted by the Los Angeles Rams in 1953, he chose instead to play for Toronto and Ottawa in the Canadian league since, unlike the NFL teams, they didn't play on Sunday. And from there, he went to seminary and on into the ministry.

Five years after speaking in Huntington, he assumed the pulpit of Bel Air Presbyterian Church in Los Angeles, where he served for nearly three decades. In 1981 and 1985, he delivered the invocation and benediction at Ronald Reagan's presidential inauguration.

The interview quoted him to say that "the nature of New Testament discipleship required that the church be missionary. When the church ceases to be redemptive, it is down and out, having no deeper fellowship than a secular or social club." He added, "Youth today want security, but they look for a false security of possessions, popularity and position. Real, lasting security comes only from being a Christian. As Christ said, 'Seek ye first the kingdom of heaven and all these things will be added unto you.' " And he called his service with Billy Graham during the London Crusade "one of the greatest experiences of my life." He subsequently made a thirty-five-thousand-mile trip around the world showing films taken of that crusade.

That semester, the religious breakdown of the student body was 27.7 percent Methodist, 27.2 percent Baptist—roughly a thousand of each—10.3 percent [generic] "Protestant," 9.9 percent Presbyterian, 6.9 percent Roman Catholic, 5.8 percent "No Preference," 4 percent Church of Christ, 2.7 percent Episcopal, and the rest at 1 percent or below (Lutheran, Church of God, Nazarene, Jewish, Greek Orthodox, Mormon, and Other). Incidentally, in response to a request from B'nai B'rith, President Smith said, in a 1956 letter, that the university would stop asking for an applicant's "religion" in its admissions forms.

Yes, the *Chimes* could be a bit edgy: SCA President Dick Kyle assured readers, in the March 1–5 issue, that the organization "does not offer a frothy swirl of emotionalism and sentimentality, but rather a wholesome devotional experience which tends to build spiritual equipoise and makes every day more meaningful." And elsewhere, in the April 16 issue, he wrote,

> Students on Marshall College campus who hold Christian principles seem to be a source of irritation to many other students and even in some cases, to the professors. This is good. There are plenty of self-styled theologians among us, who seem to have all the answers, all of which are negative. It bothers these people to be confronted with someone who is sure of his faith. If the Christian student is not careful, he will unconsciously begin to re-adjust his faith and beliefs so that they do not irritate. This is not good.

So he apparently sought to steel students against the blandishments of teachers determined to free their wards from the bonds of Sunday School faith (an enterprise, which is a cliché on countless campuses).

While Dick Kyle could speak tartly, Tom Ross, the assistant editor for the March 12 issue, offered a more devotional piece, "Moral of Life's Storms":

> Do not mourn what you've lost,
> Cursing each and every frost,
> But exalt that which you gain,
> Little can be done while you complain.
>
> The storm that seems to deluge man,
> Is just a part of God's great plan,
> The clouds that seem to bring distress,
> Give man new courage to possess.
>
> The sorrows that do work him woe,
> Stir him to bravely onward go,
> Onward in His name we proudly bear,
> To know that if we fail, He will still care.
>
> Onward to see in everything we do,
> A chance to do some kindness true,
> To serve the Lord as He wills,
> To strive to cure man's gravest ills.
>
> And thus we'll serve the Lord on high,
> Whose boundless love saves you . . . and I!

Pastor Cox's Appeal and Exhortation

In a Christmas-season issue of *The Campus Chimes* (December 17, 1958), local minister, James A. Cox of Central Christian Church, was given the front page to explain "What the Church Expects of College Students." He wrote

> . . . In many instances through casual attitudes and lukewarm interest, students decide to "sleep in" on Sunday morning and eventually relegate the church to a secondary role in their personal life. This is a grave error. These are formative years. Yet the church does not sit in judgment on the college young man and woman. We must share the blame. The church has not always manifest[ed] its interest nor made adequate provision for a comprehensive program whereby our youth may feel legitimately a part of its Christian fellowship. [E]ssentially, this is what the church asks of you.

1. That you be interested in your church and that you seek through its guidance a growing concept of God in your life.

2. That you be conscientious in your attendance at worship, study and Christian fellowship.

3. That you share with the church your talents and abilities. Be useful.

4. Be enthusiastic about your church. Believe in its precepts. Transmit your enthusiasm to others. Bring others with you.

5. Share in the stewardship of your church. The amount is not important. The fact that you are developing a rightful sense of stewardship with your God is.

6. Be a seeking, growing, creative, constructive Christian.

CCW's "Red Carpet"

Tom Ross took over as editor of *Campus Chimes*, and Sandra Roush became CCW president, having attended a summer work camp in New Mexico run by the Evangelical United Brethren. In the October, 1959 issue, Ross penned a front-page introduction to campus ministry, "Rolling Out Religion's Red Carpet."

Religion's red carpet is being rolled out to you—the class of 1963—by Marshall's Campus Christian Fellowship. Religion's red carpet is finely woven. Each thread is a vital part of the weave, holding the whole rug together, just as each student in the Campus Christian Fellowship is interwoven into the warmth of Christian brotherhood, holding the whole fellowship together.

Religion's red carpet has its red color reflected in the coals of a campfire, around which the Campus Christian Fellowship gathers for worship at a mountain retreat. At such a time, inspiration weaves our spirits together, and we feel the woven quality of our fellowship.

Religion's welcome carpet is red—a bright color—to show our bright hopes for construction of the new chapel, for a successful year of programs, and for our new study groups. But the red also stands for suffering: the blood red of the Crucifixion of Christ, whom we follow.

Religion's red carpet has spiral patterns of gray, like the roundabout pattern of the gray matter of our brains [which] follows when we discuss religion in a midnight dormitory bull session.

Religion's red carpet is soft, to ease the harness of our difficult college adjustments; it is plush, to uplift our poor spirits; and it is even worn in spots, to challenge us to work on Campus Christian Fellowship committees.

Many have walked on religion's red carpet: dean's list students and flunkers, student body presidents and campus do-nothings, science majors and religion majors, faculty members and local citizens, commuters and campus dwellers, Catholics and Jews and Protestants. All have been profoundly affected.

George and Mary walked on religion's red carpet. Mary walked on it and found herself with the Fellowship's special projects group with whom she helped the most darling orphans celebrate Christmas. Later, she followed religion's red carpet in to Rev. Beal's office, where she found friendly advice on Christian dealings with the complex moral aspects of campus dating.

George walked down religion's red carpet in to the Science Hall Auditorium, where a program featuring Greeks, Independents, and unaffiliates helped him decide whether to pledge a social group. George's activity on religion's red carpet revealed his leadership ability, for soon, the whole campus recognized him as the livewire of the Fellowship's publicity committee.

Will you walk on religion's red carpet? It will be rolled out for you at every Campus Christian Fellowship meeting, including our Thursday night sessions at 6:30 P.M. in the Science Hall Auditorium.

> Students see a hill in college:
> A mountain of God's own knowledge,
> He mines God's knowledge from that hill,
> Dare he dig deep into God's will?

Student/Campus Christian Center

Completed in 1961, the Student Christian Center (later named the Campus Christian Center), was built at a cost of $250,000, money raised through a massive crusade organized to reach four sectors—alumni, business and industry, students, and those at large.[29] The crusade chairman, department store executive Roscoe P. Mann, called it "one of the greatest projects that has ever been conducted in [the] great city of Huntington." Mann, a Methodist, served alongside six other executive committee members, drawn from a variety of denominations—Baptist, Church of God, Congregational, Disciples of Christ, Episcopal, and Presbyterian.

A planning document, "Student Participation in Religious Activities," noted that some groups declined to join in the project. There were only ten Jewish students on campus at the time, and the Catholics were not interested in participating. Nevertheless, the chapel would be open to all by petition for particular events. The overarching rationale for the undertaking: "The chapel is needed because Christ needs to be brought to the campus."

The promotional material included words of commendation from campus "religious counselor," Lander Beal (addressing "the great challenge . . . to create an atmosphere conducive to Christian decisions"); crusade board member, Andrew R. Bird (noting the seven hundred pastoral "conferences" involving Lander Beal in the previous year, observing that "every Christian churchman will be interested in giving generously to this worthy cause"); executive committee member Paul O. Fiedler (claiming that "development of fully balanced men and women requires attention to the spiritual as well as material aspects of living," and that this "training to be most effective should be done in the formative years of youth"); and student body president, Dave Kirk (declaring that a "well rounded education" called for the "development of the social, mental, physical and religious aspects of life," which the center would address, adding, "I feel the Student Body is very much in favor of this Chapel being built on the campus for their use.")

As for design, it "[departed] from traditional Cathedral form, without loss of identity as a place of worship." Indeed, the "symbols of Christian faith [were] so interspersed as to provide a unified whole with spiritual implication at every turn." Center director, Lander Beal, added, "This is truly a pilot project. It is being watched from all over the United States, since it is the only one being financed by cooperating denominations." As it turned out, the building was "a multiple purpose facility, serving not only as a house of worship but also as a place for weddings, receptions, lectures and seminars.[30]

Though some donations were substantial, Mrs. C. B. Conner of Hurricane, West Virginia, contributed a single dollar accompanied by a compelling letter (and, of course, President Smith's reply was gracious). She began by saying that she'd intended to give a hundred dollars to a scholarship fund, but circumstances had changed:

> [B]ad luck has overtaken our family so I'll enclose $1.00 [to help pay for] any of your church grounds. My younger son's home

burned to the ground a few days ago, with all contents. Nothing
at all left [except for] the clothes they were wearing. New ice box,
cook stove, electric sewing machine, TV set, spinet piano, clothes,
beddings and all—so I feel like what spare change I have now, I
have to assist them. I am sorry I can't send you more for your new
church building, or whatever you feel you need ... most ... I love
Marshall ...

Summarizing the role of the CCC, the 1964 yearbook positioned this
poem on a two-page spread of photos:

Within the Campus Christian Center,
Lives the Christian spirit or our campus;
Here, students and faculty,
Learn to recognize their responsibility under God;
It is a building full of the spirit of working together
As Christians during the day-to-day life of the University;
A place to voice questions and talk of faith;
A house of Christian truth and study.

Life-Planning Week

An annual leadership conference was held in August at Cliffside near
Charleston, and later at Cedar Lakes in Jackson County, near Ripley. Also,
Life Planning Week, with strong religious emphasis, was in vogue for a decade (1955–1965). Along the way, Beale and his committees sought ways
to boost its strength (e.g., with a big-name speaker; with "gab lab" breakout
groups; with a scheduling shift or name change), but it was ultimately replaced by a more secular program called Impact, which addressed itself to
the social issues of the 1960s.[31]

A *Chimes* issue from the Life Planning Week's heyday projected twenty-five speakers from Huntington and the surrounding communities, folks
enlisted for classroom presentations, fireside chats, and personal conferences, each assigned to address elements of social, intellectual, and religious growth. Another report (from the March 12, 1959 *Chimes*) provided
brief notes on recent LPW talks—a Methodist pastor's urging "concrete-
ness of conscience"; a UK sociology professor's connecting conscience with
dating and other social environments; a rabbi's insisting on the constant
examination and sharpening of conscience; a naval chaplain's reflections on
his calling to "make better men despite war" and not to "make the sailors

he counseled better fighters"; and President Smith's recommendation for a "philosophy of dynamic, cooperative Christianity."

Infelicities, Transgressions, and Eruptions

Not everything was idyllic in those days:

> There is no denying that the Marshall miscreants committed a variety of misdemeanors and, indeed, and occasional felony, which cut a broad swath across the spectrum of the West Virginia Civil and Criminal Code. Lesser offenses of which they were found guilty included beating bongo drums late at night, throwing Jell-O in the cafeteria, smearing paint in the Student Union, alerting fire alarms and detonating cherry bombs in the dormitory. As for "sins of the flesh," there were the usual drunken brawls, "peeping Tom" incidents and acts of indecent exposure—sometimes called "streaking." Several were pronounced guilty of committing fornication in the Donald Court apartments. Civil crimes included shoplifting in Huntington and Ashland stores, forgery, misusing vending machines, cashing bad checks and even stealing a dormitory bed.
>
> Perhaps the most heinous crime ever perpetrated by a Marshall student occurred at 11:40 a.m. on July 29, 1950, when a student robbed the First National Bank of Kenova. The young felon had escaped in a fiery red sedan, only to be apprehended 10 minutes later at Camden Park, less than two miles from the scene of the crime. The sentence imposed upon the culprit was a term in federal prison.

And then there was the student suspended in 1953 "for committing assault and battery against a professor in the classroom."[32]

Correspondence to and from President Smith and deans Buskirk and Willey reflected the normal affairs of moral housekeeping—regarding shoplifting at a local clothing store; obnoxious behavior on a chartered bus to a basketball game in Ohio; "excessive drinking, necking, lewd skits and signs ... and the 'brawl' atmosphere" at parties; cheating on a final exam by means of a note-filled index card; and drunkenness in a girls dorm. In one case, the offender got away with it, but wrote to the president several years later to say that her cheating in a particular class was bothering her, and she wanted to make things right. And, of course, the wear and tear of college life took a heavy toll on the spirits of some, including a young woman who, having been "ditched" by her boyfriend, took an overdose of sleeping pills. When Dean Buskirk came to her dorm room, the girl's "face was rather rigid and her eyes were dull," and she was sent home with her father and to a doctor's care.

On another front, there was a dustup over course readings:

> There were several liberal publications prescribed by Marshall professors that were deemed objectionable by certain obscurantic clerics in the community; yet President Smith's resolution of this issue was entirely different from that of former President Shawkey, who had been confronted with a similar problem. Attempts were made (in 1947) to suppress such liberal periodicals as *The New Republic* and *The Nation*, both of which were on the collateral reading list (though they were not actually required) of students in the Political Science Department. The local chapter of the Knights of Columbus and several clerical leaders of St. Joseph's Roman Catholic parish protested the inclusion of these magazines because of their alleged anti-Catholic bias. Since the church hierarchy had officially censored these publications, the local Catholic leaders requested that they be declared verboten by the department of political science. Dr. Smith contended, however, that: "it is the right of those instructors to choose the material which they believe will be most effective. Unless they possess that freedom," he said, "unrestricted inquiry . . . becomes a mockery." Suffice to say, the reading materials were not forbidden to the students.[33]

Finally, it's surprising to see the Minstrel Show extant in 1957, but it gets a full-page, five-photo spread in the 1957 annual. A production of the Men's Concert Choir and Omicron Delta Kappa, it generated "a load of laughs," and "the student anticipation of seeing the men's burlesque runs high, and their waiting is rarely disappointed." The biggest photo featured a professor and several students in blackface over this caption:

> The Minstrel Show's mainstay has been the endmen. They would come in between the acts of the other performers, tell jokes that would range all the way from the slightly indiscreet to the most ridiculous. The free attitude with which the endmen play their parts gives the show a flavor distinctly its own. Normally quiet and unassuming, Walter Felty (right) of the faculty defies description as a silly person in the show. One orange he threw into the audience was thrown back at him.

Mercifully, the minstrel theme was jettisoned after this performance in favor "a variety type program to give the show a wider range of possibilities."

Freshman Orientation and *motive*

In a 1957 letter to Dean Lillian Buskirk, President Smith recalled, "[A]bout a year ago I spoke favorably about the magazine "Motive" [published lower-case as *motive*] as resource material for teachers of Freshman Orientation classes." He went on, "After receiving them for several months, I have changed my estimate of it. Except for the September issue which dealt with college freshmen and an occasional article, the magazine is devoted almost entirely to articles of a religious nature. I feel that the magazine's contents are not broad enough to be of much help in our orientation classes."

"Religious nature," indeed, for *motive* was the "magazine of the Methodist Student Movement, an agency affiliated with the World's Student Christian Federation through the United Student Christian Council, published Monthly, October through May, by the Division of Educational Institutions of the Board of Education of The Methodist Church." Begun in 1941 and discontinued in 1972, when the United Methodist Church pulled the plug, it was much celebrated "for its *avant garde* editorial and artistic vision." Indeed, in 1966 *Time* magazine said it stood out among church publications "like a miniskirt at a church social." (Helpfully, the Boston University School of Theology has made a photo archive of the issues spanning those decades and posted them online.)[34]

Playing off a January 10, 1955, *Time* report on national religiosity in, *motive* offered this dialogue:[35]

> PROFESSOR: Hmmmm, 96 per cent of the U.S. citizens believe in God.
>
> CITIZEN: Not a bad record, eh?
>
> PROF: It's according to whose record you're examining: Gallup's or God's.
>
> CIT: I don't get you.
>
> PROF: Gallup counts the noses, or I should say "the ayes," And God counts the hearts.
>
> CIT: They ought to be the same number.
>
> PROF: Ought to but . . . I suppose if you asked a Methodist clergy-man if he believed in God, he'd say yes. And I'd expect the loudest

affirmatives would be from some preachers among the two hundred persons who got together in Birmingham to oppose any proposals "that seek to change the present Methodist system of separate jurisdictions for white and Negro churches."

CIT: What's that got to do with it?

PROF: I'm not going to be the judge; I just wonder if God's record is not a little confused in finding belief in his person and belief in Jim Crow on the same page—right next to Brotherhood Month too.

And another. In May of 1956, *motive* ran "The Question of Religious Life on Campus," by Nancy Green, "a student at a large midwest university." She argued that campus ministers were woefully incompetent in dealing with the tough questions students could raise—"One of the greatest difficulties of college students is the feeling that religion is asking them to believe something which is not true. They are being asked to take something wholly upon faith without the privilege of asking questions and applying the same sort of rigid intellectual tests they apply to every other area of life and thought." She was pleased to announce, "I have questioned and discarded organized religion. I have been lucky and have found something to replace these discarded beliefs . . ." By her lights, less fortunate students "have a kindergarten concept of God; and what is worse they are spiritually illiterate." Their "religion is based far too much upon outdated scientific assumptions and dogma." So she'd moved on, saying, "[B]ecause my needs have not being met by any of the organized religions which I have investigated, I am still 'shopping' I am looking for a group or a congregation who will discuss religious matters honestly." (And this from a Methodist publication.)

While President Smith was queasy over the amount of religious talk in this magazine, it's reasonable to think that the faithful in the Methodist pews would be even more relieved to have "their" publication taken off the Marshall freshman reading list. And this was still the 1950s. The magazine was just getting warmed up. When the Methodists finally shut her down in 1972, the two closing issues were built around the themes, "Lesbian/Feminist" and "Gay Men's Liberation." By the soon-to-be-unemployed editors' account, the big trouble started with the March-April 1969 double issue on "the liberation of women."

It's instructive that Dean Buskirk was keen to have in it the orientation curriculum in the first place.

Et Cetera

Campus literary magazines are typically venues for going counter-cultural in more or less artful ways. As Peter Gay aptly put it in his book title, *Modernism: The Lure of Heresy,* and as he illustrated it generously through the art of Baudelaire, Beckett, Wolff, Duchamp, Picasso, Warhol, Ray, Joyce, Stravinsky, etc., there is great contemporary cachet in being novel, cynical, and iconoclastic. You get a bit of that in the 1960 edition of *Et Cetera* in John William Teel's poem, "Christmas, 1944 (an ex-mas card)," which begins:

> And all through the house
> were strung tanks and cannons
> and battleships and planes
> and all the other children's toys
> to commemorate the holy day.
> The night before, a tired old man,
> unshaven, fat, all dressed in blood,
> brought a prosperous year to a toy company in Peoria.

And then Jean Battlo's "Autumn Agnostic," which starts

> It is easy to say there is a God—
>   but who kills trees,
>   pray, who kills trees?

The Fifties Nonetheless

Though Teel and Battlo had one foot in the fifties, they were already savoring what would become spirit of the sixties. But back in the 1956 issue, we find this more edifying piece by Sue Ripley, under the title, "Truth of Faith":

> Looking about us in this world,
>   Of what are we to think:
> Of God in his great firmament,
>   Or of the Missing Link? . . .
>
> You say you cannot believe in God,
>   The Master of us all;
> But, when a power you do seek, upon whom
>   Do you call—the first Neanderthal . . .

Although God made us from a clod,
    That is not all we are;
The immortal soul that in us dwells
    Lives on beyond a star.

Of those days, Dotty Johnson (then a Marshall prof) remembers the spiritual vitality evident in Huntington and in their church, First Presbyterian. In 1952, she and her husband Bos had fifty-five students in their college class, and, as she recalls, there was a revival among high schoolers in the city.[36]

6

Woodstock Days

WOODSTOCK, IN AUGUST OF 1969, did not spring from nothing, nor did its mythic power end when the four hundred thousand attendees left dairy farmer Sam Yasgur's pasture a soggy, trash-strewn mess. The performers had made their first recordings in the notorious sixties—Janice Joplin (1964); Jimmy Hendrix (1964); Sly and the Family Stone (1967); The Grateful Dead (1965); Joan Baez (1960); and Canned Heat (1965). In a sense, the sixties planted the seeds of Woodstock and the seventies harvested the fruit.

As Boston University professor Bruce Schulman put it,

> The Seventies transformed American economic and cultural life as much as, if not more than, the revolutions in manners and morals of the 1920s and the 1960s. The decade reshaped the political landscape more dramatically than the 1930s. In race relations, religion, family life, politics, and popular culture, the 1970s marked the most significant watershed of modern U.S. history.

He extends the borders of the revolution a bit more saying that "during the long 1970s, fifteen-malaise- and mayhem-filled years from 1969 to 1984, the United States experienced a remarkable makeover. Its economic outlook, political ideology, cultural assumptions, and fundamental social arrangement changed."[37] The changes came on with such force that the nation had something of a Darwinian Moment, a national "Scopes Trial," when people had to choose between the "Darrow" of Jimmy Hendrix and the "Bryan" of Billy Graham. And Marshall University was no exception.

Et Cetera

Well into the sixties—and in the spirit of the age—the 1968 editor of *Et Cetera*, James R. Pack, offered up a snarky take on church, under the title, "Good Advice—2." It does have the ring of an Old Testament prophet's denunciation—a jeremiad, if you will—but it's not clear whether Pack had the spiritual credentials to deliver it. Either way, it has a Woodstock tone:

> Smile, sapient theologian, lest your expert logic
> Inhibit spiritual progress.
> What can a ruse of authenticity accomplish
> If everyone knows how falsely restrictive
> Are the principles of worship?
> A godless religion would certainly suit most parishoners [sic],
> Though I doubt whether a poll would ascertain
> The extent of decay about that core.
> Can you deliver any finer eulogy to their glory
> Than boast of the size of a sanctuary,
> Cluttered with shiny ornaments and polished crosses
> Stationed at appropriate positions of respect?
> I'm pleased to note your progress toward the respectable
> Stained-glass case of splendid isolation.
> Have you always had aspirations for immortality?

Indignant *Chimes*

With the third year of publication, 1960–61, *The Chimes* took a more judgmental turn under the editorship of Rule Johnson, the new student senate chaplain. He was taken with such Beat Generation writers as Seymour Krim (who wrote for the *Village Voice* and *Playboy*) and the poet Lawrence Ferlinghetti, who was co-founder of City Lights bookstore in San Francisco, site of the aforementioned reading of "Howl."

He ran a Krim piece, "Making It!" with the introduction,

> The Christian Church becomes most nearly the Redemptive Community of Christ when it is neither defensive nor rejective to attack of this nature, but rather seeks a dialogue with those outside her Fellowship. We print this work and pose three questions: DOES THIS ACCURATELY REFLECT THIS GENERATION/ WHAT DOES THE CHRISTIAN GOSPEL SAY TO "MAKING IT!"; IF MR. KRIM ENTERED YOUR CHURCH FELLOWSHIP, HOW

WOULD YOU DEMONSTRATE TO HIM THE UNIQUENESS
OF THE REDEMPTIVE CHRISTIAN FELLOWSHIP?

And so from Mr. Krim:

> In every brain cell of intellectual and artistic life the heat is on
> in America today no differently than it is in business. Values?
> Purpose? Selectivity? Principles? For the birds, Charley! I want to
> make it and nothing's going to stand in my way because every-
> thing is crap except making it! Be honest, for Godsakes. I want
> my ego to ride high, my heart to bank the loot of my life, my MG
> to snarl down the highway, my pennant to wave above the broken
> dreams for a better world! Why don't you level and say you want
> the same, you hypocrite?
>
> The only enemy today is failure, failure, and the only true
> friend is—success! How? In what line? Whoring yourself a little?
> Buttering up, sucking up, self-salesmanship, the sweet smile? Don't
> be naïve, friend. You think this hallucinated world is the moon-
> light sonata or something? You think anyone cares about your
> principles of (don't make me puke!) integrity or that they make
> the slightest ripple in the tempest of contemporary confusion? Go
> sit at home, then, you plastic saint and keep pure like the monks,
> because if you want to make it in the world, baby, you have to
> swing, move, love what you hate, and love yourself for doing it too!
> . . . while down below the lusting average man and woman sweats
> in jealousy at the sight of these doxodrene [neologism, riffing on
> dexedrine?] angels, the very inspiration of what he and she can
> become if only they, too, can put the last shred of shame behind
> them and swing, extrovert yourself, get with it, make that buck,
> make that chick, make that poem, make this crazy modern scene
> pay off, O my heart, so I can too can sink my teeth in the sirloin
> and wear the pearls of hell!

If you listen closely, you can hear the dismay/disgust of Dustin Hoffman's character (Benjamin Braddock) in *The Graduate* over the career tip
from Mr. McGuire—"Plastics." And so the sixties were upon us. (Incidentally, Rule Johnson's 1961 yearbook picture for *The Chimes* shows him with
close-cropped hair, a three-piece suit, white shirt, and a pocket handker-
chief, with a visage not unlike that of Jim Parsons in *The Big Bang Theory*.)

(It turns out that those with the Seymour Krim/Benjamin Braddock
perspective were just getting warmed up. In a full-page screed in the 1973
yearbook, across from a full-page photo of its writer, graduate student Rich
Hensley, the reader is treated to sweeping dismissal of those interested in

success in the corporate world. These are the souls susceptible to the counsel to "maintain vigilance over your subordinates, remembering that those bastards are after YOUR job." The end point, according to Hensley: "Having divested yourself of your background, friends, family, and individuality, the only thing of substance left in your life is the Firm." And so you may be rewarded "with a vice-presidency and stock options. And you will have 'made it.' Congratulations.")

The February, 1964 *Chimes* issue ("Pealing the Tone of Marshall College's Religious Activity") was full of invective, particularly over civil rights. Mary Sue Allen's front page poem, "We're Here, But Where is Here?" begins with

> No, this isn't America,
> Not the place of freedom.
> Else why can I not
> Eat with other men?

Reading on, we find political science professor Paul Stewart discussing *Plessy v. Ferguson* ("separate-but-equal accommodation"); an apocalyptic parable by D. Hammon, with such prose as "Fear is the bastard brother of hate; these are born from the whore Ignorance and fathered by the Idoit [sic] Stupidity"; excerpts from MLK's "Letter from a Birmingham Jail"; and observations by philosophy prof, Lloyd Beck (e.g., "In the arena of realistic politics laws often emerge which are compromising and discriminatory. They are concessions to expediency.").

Another *Chimes* issue offered a review of the play, *The Sign of Jonah*, set in post WWII Berlin and translated from the German. It was "surrealistic," featuring a play within a play within a play, and it worked with both "religious beliefs and modern psychological concepts." And another issue ran a Lawrence Ferlinghetti poem, "Christ Climbed Down" ("from His bare Tree this year and ran away to where there were no rootless Christmas trees hung with candy canes and breakable stars").

So they'd moved on from the Frank Laubach and Don Moomaw style of early issues.

President Smith's Report

Drawing from President Smith's notes for a December 6, 1965 talk at the Huntington Ministerial Association, we learn that, before his coming in

1949, there were only six student religious organizations on campus—
Episcopal (Canterbury), Jewish (Hillel), Catholic (Newman), Baptist,
Methodist, Lutheran—all led by local church staff. Early on, he suggested
a "Religious Emphasis Week" on campus, an idea which emerged as "Life
Planning Week," where there would be "no preaching or exhortive [sic]
lectures." Rather, students and leaders would "discuss some of Life's most
perplexing problems franking and informally," thus to "develop a finer
sense of values" through these discussions.

Dean Buskirk's Assessment

Lillian Buskirk was dean of women at Marshall from 1941 to 1970. West
[residence] Hall was renamed in her honor in 1976. In a 1965 paper, "Mood
of the Campus," prepared for a higher education symposium, she reflected
on the spiritual and cultural tone of the school and ventured some suggestions, both for those days and for the future.[38]

In her own student years, she was involved with the Christian Endeav-
or Society and in the paper, she spoke freely of the need "to find our unity of
oneness in Christ." She was very concerned over the dehumanizing effects
of the world and was keen to see the church and campus ministry cooperate
in making Christianity "relevant." She recounted the non-denominational
efforts of the early twentieth century, including the strong work of the Y.
("The earlier so-called appointment of Dean of Men and Dean of Women
were essentially YMCA secretaries with offices in the university.") But then
she acknowledged and embraced the rise of denominational interests, with
the corresponding need for cooperation among these groups, working together with the school. She began,

> The mood of the Marshall campus is changing—as it is on all other
> campuses of the U.S., but—in my opinion, to a much lesser degree.
> I believe this is true of all W. Va. Campuses. Why? . . . The search
> for religious liberty led the pioneer settlers, primarily Quakers,
> Dunkards and Mennonites to West Virginia. Although these
> "plain people" have left the state their influence may still be noted.
> Hugh Maxwell in his West Virginia and Its People says that today
> we find the southern miner holding tenaciously to the ideas of his
> fathers in religion; the hillbilly, while rejecting newfangled edu-
> cational theories for his young, is convinced of man's inheritance
> of the image of God . . . From the small communities from which
> we draw over half of our students it is not uncommon to find

public baptisms, camp meetings, prayer meetings in homes and evangelistic meetings in which the entire community takes part. The church for some and the little restaurant—"beer garden"—for the others are the social centers. The religious beliefs are stern and many times accompanied by primitive manifestations.

After taking her cultural readings from the Maxwell book, she turns to the World Student Christian Federation publication, "The University in the Academic World," for guidance:

> [I]t dawned on me that perhaps what we need to say . . . [is that higher education] is becoming more and more the pivotal center of society structure; that we see it as an instrument of God for the changes that must and that will occur in society structure. God is already working his work, in the academic world. The church may well have to rethink its concern, to regard the public domain—the secular world so to speak—as encompassing the world of creation which is under God. This takes on a new aspect, new consideration, as to how we relate and how we witness and how to work in its midst. No longer are we threatened by the university today as once we were in the early twenties. I recall the time when even I was told, "Don't go to a state institution. You will lose all your faith. Don't you take philosophy . . . that will weaken your faith". I don't think we are fooled with that kind of a dogmatical or authoritarian consideration.

She offers a word of caution, though: "[W]e see cries for freedom from every segment of our society. But the use of it is not just to end it here for that ends in anarchy." But the happy prospect of properly-bounded schooling is within our reach: "Liberal education is liberal, liberating, if it can cope with the humanization process to make people persons, to act within their own right and understanding, to equip them so that they can be the reconciling force in their society, in our society."

(Perhaps the good dean would be less sanguine today at the performance of American universities in inculcating the best that the church had to offer to society.)

Racial Integration

Turning through President Smith's 1960s correspondence in the archives, one finds him and his administration addressing a range of misbehaviors and conflicts—dorm noise making a pre-pharmacy student "a nervous wreck," as he tried to sleep and study; a student stashing cherry bombs in his own dorm room; theft of a dorm bunk bed for use in a private apartment; the noisy partying of Alpha Sigma Phi (with drums and unchaperoned girls in the fraternity house), which ran till 3:30 in the morning and disturbed the Sixth Avenue neighbors; upset in some quarters over the requirement that students receiving NDEA (National Defense Education Act) grants sign a loyalty oath, one disavowing sympathy or connections with groups teaching "the overthrow of the United States Government by force or violence or by any illegal or unconstitutional methods."

But the most sweeping concern was discrimination against black students, and Smith was involved in its amelioration. Use of the racially segregated Keith-Albee Theater was particularly problematic since it was "the only local auditorium which has a satisfactory place for the Artists Series, Baccalaureate Service and Commencement." For Smith's labors, the local, black Professional and Business Men's Club gave him and Rabbi Levy credit for working alongside the NAACP and church leaders in putting pressure on that establishment—an estimated two thousand man hours of effort from all parties involved. They noted, "In all instances, the appeals have been based on persuasion, the dignity of the individual, inalienable God-given rights, etc."

In a letter to the group, Smith recalled various efforts to address the situation—securing an invitation to the black Douglass High School (named for Frederick Douglass) to participate in the high school band festival; persuading the Huntington Hotel to house visiting teams with black players; conferencing with local store and restaurant managers to nudge them toward accommodation, only to hear that they couldn't comply since they needed to "protect their investments."

Four years after the Civil Rights Act, the University's Human Relations Committee dealt with a case of discrimination in the local Modern Café. On July 14, 1968, a white student, Ross Frye, went to the establishment with an African student, John Ndege, and was refused service. When he returned that evening to ask why, the owner was surprised to hear that Ndege was a foreign student, saying he thought he was "an American negro," as if that mattered.

In February of that year, Herbert Henderson, president of the West Virginia chapter of the NAACP, had come to speak at the CCC. His assessment, covered by *The Parthenon* (February 14) was grim: "Negroes are not accepted in total Marshall University school life." For one thing, "lily-white" fraternities and sororities should start accepting students on their individual merits rather than excluding them on the basis of race. He warned, "Unless white people change, there will be another long hot summer all across the country," predicting that whites would eventually change because they didn't want their cities destroyed.

An August 31, 1962 letter from the state Human Rights Commission shows how things have changed regarding the desideratum, "color blindness," which drove the Civil Rights Movement. The ideal was encapsulated in Martin Luther King's 1963 speech at the Lincoln Memorial: "I have a dream that my four little children will one day live in a nation where they will not be judged by the color of their skin but by the content of their character." The commission showed which state schools had transgressed by asking, in application forms, for race, religion, and nationality—and for a photo. Bluefield State, Fairmont State, Potomac State, Shepherd, and West Virginia State were the worst offenders, but the commission was pleased that these schools had agreed to remove these requests.

This has a quaint cast to it since, today, the government requires "diversity and inclusion" reports for schools desiring funding. The Office of Management and Budget uses for evaluation, the categories, "White, Black or African American, American Indian or Alaska Native, Asian, and Native Hawaiian or Other Pacific Islander." (Incidentally, to complicate matters, studies have shown that first names alone can signal racial categories, with 'Jamal' signaling more than 'John.') Be that as it may, the "color blind" criterion of that 1962 commission was arguably admirable.

Incidentally, *The Parthenon* (November 6, 1968) reported that seventeen Marshall students interrupted a city hall speech by Senator Robert Byrd (who, at his death in 2010, was the longest-serving member of Congress in the nation's history) by standing and singing "We Shall Overcome" and by parading down the aisle with signs reading, "MU students abhor racism" and "Byrd, KKK Wallace." He was in town for a political rally, with about five hundred people in attendance, and the students' performance was not well received. Leaving the auditorium, they formed up on the sidewalk outside and sang "The Battle Hymn of the Republic." Their complaint was that Byrd was an officer of the Klan back in the forties, an association he later, in 1993, called "the greatest mistake I ever made."

The (Ecumenical) Community

In 1966, the Christian Community at Marshall [the ecumenical core of campus ministry], with headquarters in the Campus Christian Center, updated their "Articles of Operations and Bylaws" for the purpose of "moving toward a deeper dimension" among those committed to "the expression of oneness among those who profess the Lordship of Jesus Christ, in order to present the gospel with integrity on the campus." To this end, "participating persons" would subscribe to the following:

> The basis of The Community is the faith attested by the holy Scriptures and affirmed in the confessions and the life of The Church, that God incarnate in Jesus Christ and present in the Holy Spirit wills to reconcile men to himself, and that he is acting in history, creating, judging, and redeeming.
>
> We affirm that in The Church of Jesus Christ we are members of one body and we believe that we are called to this one expression of our ministry as a more adequate expression of our unity in The Church, that we may better proclaim the Gospel, and join ourselves to what God is doing, in campus and community life.

Furthermore, they would adhere to the covenant, which included these items:

> To receive the nurture of The Church and at the same time to enable The Community to be a prophetic voice within the life of the churches, pioneering on all frontiers of faith and work;
>
> To increase sensitivity to and understanding of the responsibilities of Christians within the university and to help the university become more fully itself;
>
> To increase the sensitivity to and understanding of the responsibility to which God calls members of the academic community in the political, economic, and social world . . .
>
> To deepen our understanding of and participation in the expressions of unity in the life of The Church especially through the National Student Christian Federation and the World Student Christian Federation . . .
>
> To participate with any groups whose aims in particular situations seems Christian.

And then, among the responsibilities enumerated by The Community: "It shall explore, pursue and be involved in continuing ecumenical strategy" and attend to "interpretation to the various denominations of The Church's ministry in higher education."

(Over the years, the World Student Christian Federation has morphed into an essentially progressive/liberal organization, with focus upon social justice rather than evangelism. As such, it stands in contrast to more evangelical movements.)

George Sublette and the "Social Approach"

As the sixties drew to a close, new leadership emerged in the person of George Sublette. With a background in church and campus ministry, he came to Marshall as Baptist campus pastor in the 1960s and was picked as chairman of the CCC staff in the fall of 1970. He played a prominent role in shaping the campus religious scene, starting *The Voice* ("We don't expect the Parthenon or the Herald Dispatch to give their point of view concerning the CCC and we realize that sometimes our perspectives don't come through . . .") and as faculty advisor to Impact, both of which we'll visit in a moment. He also served on various "mental health" and "community action" teams in the area.

Those were busy days for the CCC, which was open daily from 8:00 a.m. to 11:00 p.m. (A 1968 survey suggested that as many as nine hundred students had attended at least one event at the center.) The October 1967 calendar shows dozens of group activities, including Catholic Mass on Sunday morning, Baptist Collegiate Ministry on Monday night, Christian Science and Christian Athlete gatherings on Tuesday morning, Episcopal "Mass" on Thursday evening, and the Proctor Project ("recreational and creative activity" for "young, underprivileged and probably unloved children of the area east and south of the campus").

In the February 6 issue, *The Parthenon* ran a piece on the CCC's mission consensus. Instead of following the "evangelistic approach" ("going door-to-door"; "jamming down the throat"), "generally the ministers feel the social approach is the most effective, realistic, and modern way." While the evangelism enthusiasts might focus on getting people into heaven, the social outreach crew resonated with Sublette's observation: "The primary purpose of the church is to make available to the people the resources of the Gospel, that is resources for living. The most important being hope. When you lose hope you stop being a person."

In an October 6, 1967 update on CCC activities, he explained that the Encounter series was a "weekly issue oriented program" dealing with such topics as "myth and the Bible" and "The Role of the Military in a Democratic society." He added, "All viewpoints have the opportunity to be heard. The WORD must engage the crucial questions." (Perhaps it is no stretch of the imagination that Sublette's starting points were the convictions that 1. the Bible relies heavily on myth—in the sense of a story not to be taken literally—as in the "Creation Myth" and the "myths" of Jonah and Job; and that, 2. that the military is a threat to democratic society.)

Campus Presbyterian minister Hardin "Corky" King added, "I suppose my goal would be to fight against the dehumanizing process within the university using every opportunity to create better understanding between persons," adding, "[W]e see our goal to be 'available', and not to give a pressing or forceful impression." So the emphasis was on dialogue and counseling. They also touted contemporary worship on campus, using jazz and formats not found in the traditional church.

To be fair, Sublette did address the beyond and the fate of souls. In an issue of *The Parthenon*, published four days after the crash ("Rev. Sublette looks at the tragedy"), he quoted from Ecclesiastes 3 ("For everything there is a season . . .") and Romans 8 ("[Nothing] will be able to separate us from the love of God in Christ Jesus our Lord"). Of course, the latter left open the question of whether those who died and those grieving were "born again" in Christ. Right along, Sublette took pains to distance himself from people who would draw lessons from the crash: "I don't know what it means! I haven't heard anybody profaning the situation by trying to get some moral out of it." It's not clear how an observation like, "It's a wakeup call, forcing us to consider whether we're ready to meet our maker" would be profane, but Sublette offered no clarification.

He was clear-spoken on a number of things, as when, in the June 17, 1971 issue, he told *The Parthenon* that the church "was involved in the ethical issues of the day . . . in the mater of peace, of ending the war, because they feel God cares about men. He loves them and war has no place in the world." (Not even to stop Hitler?) Though Sublette was a whirlwind of activity and a strong campus presence, his sending body, the American Baptist Convention (previously the Northern Baptist Convention, subsequently the American Baptist Churches, USA) was not as impressed. When *The Parthenon* asked why he was leaving Marshall in the fall of 1971, he replied, "The Baptists feel the center is hampering their denominational work. It's not a matter of money, but of philosophy."

In a postscript to Sublette's tenure, Robin Crouch (part of the original Crusade group, the man who later filled Sublette's shoes as BCM director from 1984 to 1989) recalls Sublette as a good guy, but one lacking evangelical fervor. When it came Crouch's turn to lead the group, the national, ABC/BCM material promoted protest, and he simply ignored it. Rather, characteristic of his more evangelistic focus, Crouch hosted Christian magician André Kole, who wove gospel witness into his performance as a team member with Campus Crusade for Christ.

Impact

As noted above, Life Planning Week gave way to Impact in 1965. The spring 1970 version (in the year of the plane crash) featured controversial people tasked to address "relevant" topics brewing in the day. Many of these were strictly political characters, feeding or palliating the spirit of the sixties. Paul Krasner, a founder of the New Left "Yippie" movement, was supposed to speak about "Censorship in the 70s," but ended up commending LSD to the students, many of whom walked out. (The *Parthenon* photo of this event was taken in the CCC.) Jeremy Larner, a speech writer for Senator Eugene McCarthy, urged students to work within the system for change. David Dellinger, one of the Chicago Seven (defendants charged with inciting a riot at the 1968 Democratic Convention in Chicago), had to cancel, but was replaced by John Froines, another member of that group. Tom Davis of the *Cleveland Plain Dealer* was also on the program.

The ministerial voice for Impact that year was the Rev. Malcolm Boyd, best known for his earthy prayers in *Are You Running With Me Jesus?* (with a cover picture of Boyd in clerical collar, cigarette in his mouth on the first edition). In it, he spoke of wanting to slug a white "respectable gentleman" whose clichés "crucified" Negroes; of asking Jesus to be with men in a homosexual bar, both there and in church. The book had a gritty feel to it, as in these lines:[39]

- "Today I feel like a slave bound in chains and branded by a hot iron because I'm a captive to my own will and don't give an honest damn about you [Jesus] or your will."

- "Help me to put away the tranquilizers and just be myself with you and the others you place with me."

- "I feel disengaged from life at this moment. Time has stopped, and nothing matters. I have nowhere to hurry, no place to go, no sensible goal. I might as well be dead."

- "I want to get home, Lord, but the traffic won't move . . . I'm too damned tired to be patient, and I'm hot and sweaty."

Boyd came out as gay in 1977, and the fortieth-anniversary edition of the book reflects that in a piece entitled "May we have your blessing, Jesus?":

> I come to Mark, my partner not filled with sound and fury and the
> lies of the world
> I come to him naked early morning eyes and tousled hair He
> knows my snoring my morning feet shuffling toward coffee
> I come to him as I am . . . unvarnished floor unframed picture
> and face that needs a shave a character with flaws
> May we have your blessing Jesus?[40]

His 1971 talk was also provocative. As reported in that week's *Parthenon*, he called racial integration a "cruel thing," wherein "Negroes are being forced to live white lives—the complete power structure is against the Negro"; said, "The only way to define Jesus is to act out your life through the definition you have of him"; commended the underground church as thrilling, in that it was "open to all people," "concerned with social justice," possessing "a sense of joy and celebration," and marking "a complete break with traditional authority."

This was consistent with the "in your face" tone of Impact, particularly if your face was traditional and evangelical. As John W. Masland, coordinator of the 1969 program, put it in their brochure, "[T]his is the philosophy of IMPACT—to create 'intellectual abrasion' through our ability to reason and to do this is to separate us from the beasts and will ultimately allow mankind to leave the protection of the womb." Claude W. Doak, the editor of that year's printed piece observed,

> Lest we frighten you reader, we are not asking for anything that we
> have not been given by law; the same freedoms the old "Way" has
> allowed to stagnate while our elders have had their ears so full of
> red, white and blue bunting and Bible loving conservatism that they
> could not hear the crys [sic] of the Negro, the poor, and the aged.

While they did enlist the conservative intellectual William F. Buckley (editor of *National Review*) in 1971 and the "radioactive" Robert Welch (head of the John Birch Society) in 1969, the IMPACT fare was more typically leftist—in 1968, Beat poet Allen Ginsberg, sexologist Lester Kirkendall (said to have attacked both the "Puritan right and the libertine left"), and black comedian Dick Gregory, who won a law suit the following year after he was barred from performing at the University of Tennessee. (At that school, the administration had heard that he was an "extreme racist" who would inflame the sentiments of many in that state.) At Marshall, Gregory tossed out a variety of incendiary comments, such as calling vice president Hubert Humphrey "a murderer with blood on his hands." He also ventured the prediction that, because of pollution over the next thirty to forty years [culminating between 1998 and 2008], temperatures would rise five degrees, the polar ice caps would melt, and the world would be inundated and, thus, become uninhabitable.

(Incidentally, once the 1968 Impact was a wrap, the committee surveyed the student body by questionnaire and personal interviews, gathering speaker suggestions for the future. Recommendations included Cleveland mayor Carl Stokes; writers Truman Capote, Rod McKuen, Ayn Rand, and Walter Lippman; former first lady Jacqueline Kennedy; advice columnist Abigail Van Buren; Hindu holy man Maharishi Mahesh Yogi; and nudist candidate for president, Louis Abolafia, whose campaign slogan was "What have I got to hide?")

In 1969, the roster featured Herbert Aptheker (a Marxist historian, member of the Communist Party) and Bishop James Pike (an alcoholic, censured by the Episcopal House of Bishops for such things as denying the Virgin Birth, the reality of hell, and the concept of the Trinity). Then, in the 1970s, along came Margaret Mead (anthropologist who penned the "sexual-liberation" book, *Coming of Age in Samoa*); Abbie Hoffman (another of the Chicago Seven); David Harris (imprisoned for draft-evasion, the husband of Joan Baez); George Carlin (famous for the monologue, "Seven Dirty Words You Can't Say on Television"—two of them excretory, five of them sexual); and Jonathon Round (with an album entitled *Psychedelic Rock Essentials*). Of course, all of these personalities were capable of universally admirable and thoroughly conventional activities, but it's unlikely that they were chosen for Impact on this basis. Through the years, the invited politicos were typically Democrats—George McGovern, Hubert Humphrey, Julian Bond, and Gale McGee.

One regular feature was *The Barfenon Review*, described in 1969 as a "farcical, no-holds-barred satire [depicting] scenes both at Marshall University and the nation as a whole. Named after that snake tongued journal of free and liberal thought, *The Parthenon*, *The Barfenon Revue* has shown no mercy with its cutting satire and sharp wit."

A 1971 year book entry, "Looking Ahead to the 70's," offered up a *cri de coeur* (or perhaps a word of slander) regarding disappointing attendance at Impact events:

> If the largest crowd attending any one impact event numbered somewhere around 400 people . . . And if many of these 400 people were the same ones attending all the events . . . And if these 400 people represent 5% of the entire student body . . . And if one can reasonably assume that at least a 70% of those not present did not care to come at all . . . Then one can tentatively assume that Marshall is a functioning model of typical America (silent majority vs. vocal minority). And that West Virginia can look to its future as holding the same experiences, in futility, exercises in mediocrity and experiments in fatalism that it has been saddled with for decades.

Buffalo Babes and the "Spontaneous Irritation"

In September of 1970, a "spontaneous irritation" (so called by the irritators) emerged on campus in response to the football program's plan to recruit "Buffalo Babes" to welcome prospective players to campus, show them around, and attend games with them. Coach Red Dawson was taking the lead, picking up on a program he'd seen at other schools. Though about twenty-five interested women showed up at an informational meeting, two indignant women from the campus "feminist movement" attended to voice their objections, as they had been doing throughout the day at a sidewalk display.

The rhetoric was sharp. Feminist signs read, "We didn't come to MU to 'learn' to be 'date bait' for the football team," and "MU needs you. (Women wanted to be exploited by the Athletic Department). Be a token student." Bluefield senior, Patricia O'Connor declared, "As a woman at MU my primary purpose is higher learning. It infuriates me that the sexist institution will not allow women on their sports teams and will not hire women in executive positions." Continuing with the "nuclear option," she charged, "Their audacity to attempt to use women to secure athletes is another example of this sexist institution's systematic exploitation of another n****r class—women."

In response, the non-irritated women said that they were there voluntarily, that no, they didn't feel "used," and that there were athletic options for them through Marshall's NCAA-sanctioned women's teams in softball, basketball, tennis and field hockey. This was not good enough, for O'Connor insisted that she should be allowed to participate in men's football if she so desired.

Coach Dawson was not particularly interested in diplomacy, calling the attack "silly" and saying that the one protesting "couldn't help us anyway." He said that O'Connor "had illusions of grandeur and was hypnotized by her own voice," adding that the program would "go on as planned."

The first issue of the national magazine *Ms.* was yet to appear as an insert in *New York* magazine in December 1971, but the Marshall feminists had plenty to draw on—from the 1800s (Wollstonecraft) up though the 1940s (de Beauvoir) and 1960s (Friedan), to the previous year, 1970, with works by Greer (*The Female Eunuch*), Millet (*Sexual Politics*), and Firestone (*The Dialectic of Sex*).

Of course, fifty years later, a lot of water has gone under the bridge. Title IX has boosted women's athletics while taking down school funding for some men's teams, notably in wrestling and track. Many schools still field athletic "hostesses," but they don't call them "babes." And yes, some scandals have occurred. Things, indeed, "were a'changin'" with the jury still out (or the jury irreparably hung) on which changes were salubrious and which were not.

The Voice, October 1970

It's interesting to read of the spiritual activities of 1970 noted in *The Voice*, item published on October 19, a month ahead of the crash. Little did those involved know that their faith would be tested so dramatically in short order:

- Throughout the fall, Volunteers in Community Service (VICS) utilized over two hundred students for work with Huntington area hospitals and service institutions, a program for "students interested in serving their fellow-man."

- The CCC sponsored a series of Sunday evening seminars on "The Mass Media: Creative Force in Society." Tri-state media representatives were enlisted to discuss such topics as the power of and pressures on journalists, the coverage and involvement of minorities, and the promise of public television. American Baptist campus minister,

George Sublette, said the programs would be "a significant contribution to community life in Huntington."

- The CCC sponsored an ecumenical worship service each Sunday morning, following a fellowship time over coffee and donuts. Worship was "so structured to allow much singing [accompanied by piano, string bass, guitar, autoharp, drums and other instruments], scripture readings and prayers." The aim was "to provide an experience which will enable both campus and community persons to grow in the Christian faith, to provide contemporary expression of the matters of the Christian faith for those who are struggling with a classical expression only" and "to enable participants to realize together the oneness of the family of God."

- The Howard Hanger [jazz] Trio of Atlanta was scheduled to lead the CCC's morning worship on December 13 after a coffee house performance the night before. Their aim: "By seeking to establish a sense of awareness, by attempting to break down the barriers that exist between the sacred and the secular, by using one means after another to open persons to each other, the Trio looks for the Spirit to take it from there." Sister Norma Rodriguez of the Diocese of Charleston, South Carolina was quoted: "The Trio breaks through the fringes of existence and touches their audiences at the heart of the American Christian matter. If you remain comfortable during their performance, if you remain thoughtless and emotionless and uninvolved . . . you're dead."

- Campus ministers, George Sublette (American Baptist), Corky King (Presbyterian), William Miller (Methodist), and Robert Scott (Catholic), made themselves available to various dorms for informal meetings and pastoral counseling.

- Individual articles gave backgrounds on these four men, beginning with Sublette, who had recently come as American Baptist Campus minister and who had assumed the role of chairman of the CCC staff. We read that "his primary style of ministry is that of pastoral counseling," and, in that connection, that he was vice president of the Cabell Huntington Mental Health Association and a member of the state association's board of directors. With a BA in psychology from Capital University (Ohio) and a BD from Crozer Theological Seminary (Pennsylvania), he had ministry experience at the congregational level and on campus at the University of Delaware. (Martin

Luther King also attended Crozer, which closed in 1970 in a merger with Colgate Rochester Divinity School, itself the result of a merger; her early faculty included Walter Rauschenbusch, father of the "social gospel." Today, the school proclaims, "For almost 200 years, Colgate Rochester Crozer Divinity School has served as one of the world's leading progressive theological schools, preparing socially conscious, socially active leaders who impact the world through Christ-centered leadership and service.")

- In an essay, "Free, At Last," Sublette, who was editor of *The Voice*, railed against "the ghetto and the slavery of economic and political prejudice"; against "the military machine [that] seeks to crush the human spirit" of the Palestinian Liberation movement; and against "parents, universities, and governments," seeking to "imprison [the young] within their childhood or adolescence." He praised "the post-war existentialists" who "describe well the feelings of aloneness, lostness, anxiety fear, dread, aimlessness, and depression" and also Gandhi, who "came to know the record of Jesus' life and to know him as a person" thus discovering "the freedom of the human spirit that nothing in all creation can take away."

- Hardin "Corky" King, earned a BD at Union Theological Seminary in Richmond and served as a Presbyterian campus minister at the University of Georgia, where as chaplain at Westminster House, he caught flak for befriending black students while the school was desegregating. When he came to serve Marshall in that same capacity, he also became pastor of Huntington's Green Valley Presbyterian Church.

- With a BA from West Virginia Wesleyan, a BD from Duke Divinity School, and pastoral experience in Morgantown, where he organized "Camp Daybreak for emotionally disturbed boys," William Miller came to Marshall as Methodist Campus Minister. Simultaneously, he served as pastor of Huntington's Emmanuel United Methodist Church and director of the Contact-Huntington, 24-hour crisis intervention center.

- A graduate of Holy Cross and the Paulist Fathers Seminary in Washington, D.C., Robert Scott became Marshall's first full-time Catholic chaplain. He had previously served in this capacity at West Virginia University and Ohio State.

- With degrees from West Virginia and General Theological Seminary in New York City, Ken Price occupied the joint position of Episcopal Chaplain and vicar of St. Andrew's Episcopal Church in Barboursville. His cooperative role on the CCC team was in special ministry to the "Greek Houses."

- Campus Christian Ministry started the Faculty Luncheon Forum, which continued well into the 1970s. As philosophy professor Howard Slaatte put it, the series "Does more than anything else on this campus to foster better faculty communication." For a dollar a meal, students, staff, and faculty could meet in groups of ten to "exchange thoughts on sundry current issues pertinent to campus life and beyond." Each group was organized for cross-disciplinary dialogue, with, for example, representatives from engineering, geology, the library, chemistry, speech, physics, counseling and rehabilitation, vocational technical education, WMUL-TV, and political science. Even President Roland Nelson was involved before his resignation in July, after two turbulent years in that role.

"Corky's" Doings

Pictured dashingly shirtless on a tennis court in the October 11, 1967, *Parthenon*, Hardin "Corky" King was a whirlwind of activity.

- In his April 1967 report, Campus Christian Center staff chairman, Hardin King, dealt with two criticisms—that some of the religious services (a folk mass and an "artistic collage" event) were offensive and puzzling to some, and that some were saying the CCC was "Comsymp" since most of its treatment of the Vietnam War was negative. "Corky" argued that all was well. He also said that, given the cultural blinders of the students, the CCC was offering a series of meetings, led by professors, dealing with such topics as NATO, Vietnam, nuclear weapons, and the war on hunger.

- Catching heat from the community, "Corky" sent a letter to President Smith explaining that a recent "happening" at the CCC Coffee House was licit and profound. Less sanguine was the local paper, whose account included a "figure, clothed in black" who circled the room and then sat in a corner "facing a wall and, from the light of a red bulb, read aloud from the sayings of Buddha, Mohammed, and Jesus. He was to continue his reading for two hours." Meanwhile, a graduate student robed in white with plastic flowers on his head, read "poetry and the philosophies of Zen Buddhism and Yoga" in the center of the room. A third figure "struggled for 40 minutes or more, trying to free himself [from a plastic dry cleaning bag]. He failed." Vague shapes were projected on the wall; tinsel and candles came into play; there was body painting. And so it went.

- In requesting funds for establishment of a theological library ($5,000 at the start and $500 a year for additions), he cited suggestions from *Christian Century* ("progressive, ecumenical") and Union Theological Seminary (who would soon hire liberal theologian, Paul Tillich).

- In October, 1965, President Smith, at Corky's suggestion, wrote pastors in the region, inviting them to campus for a day, so that they might get "a better 'feel' for campus life and higher education," the aim being "better rapport between pastors and the university." On March 1, 1966, the second symposium for pastors within a two-hour drive in the tri-state area, was held with nearly a hundred in attendance. Mental health was the focus.

- In 1971, two years before *Roe v. Wade* made abortion legal throughout the U.S., *The Parthenon* supported its legalization in West Virginia, and the paper was running ads for an abortion service in New York. Corky warned that some of these providers were objectionable and he suggested turning to the Clergy Consultation Service, of which he was a member. He explained, "Abortion is not necessarily the answer to every pregnancy . . . The first thing we do is work through the options presented to us, which include marriage, adoption, keeping the child yourself or with your parents. The girl decides for herself and we proceed from there."

- In September of 1971, he announced a CCC speaking visit by Carl Henry, a conservative, evangelical theologian, who, in the years to come, would be an outspoken foe of abortion. It's not clear from the *Parthenon* item King had scheduled the talks, but his publicizing them reflected the CCC policy of hosting a wide range of activities.

Miscellany

The 1961 "Manual for Student Counselors in the Men's Residence Halls" included "a person with religious convictions" in the employee description. It also said he should understand, "It is normal at this time to have some doubts about one's religious teaching." If such arose, the troubled student should be referred to the "Campus Religious Counselor or to his own Minister." Furthermore, "Encourage him to participate in our Life Planning Week. Refer him to references in our Library."

The January 26, 1967 gathering of the CCC board covered the question of whether Catholic ministry might be admitted to the program, with one member saying he didn't want that influence featured there, and another saying that though "there is ingrained in us an historical distrust in the Roman Catholic Church," he trusted the Protestant clergymen to deal with any problems," observing that the "coming together must be done in small steps, and each step honestly considered."

7

Four Spiritually Impactful Professors

IN ITS NEARLY TWO centuries of existence, Marshall has employed thousands of professors. (Howard Moffat's history lists almost seventeen hundred between 1920 and 1980.) All of them, whether short or long term, have had an impact, many of them momentous. Here is a sampler of four who are connected particularly to the book's theme.

Howard Slaatte and Mainline Protestantism

Howard Slaatte succeeded Lloyd Beck as chairman of the philosophy department in 1966, and he brought to the campus a rich blend of Wesleyan theology and philosophy, particularly in the work of Nicholas Berdyaev.

Berdyaev is typically termed a "Christian existentialist." His focus was on the freedom and creativity of the individual, accountable to God and not the state, so he early on found himself at odds with the totalitarian nature of the Soviet Union. Expelled along with other troublesome intellectuals in 1922, he settled near Paris, where he worked until his death in 1948. (Alexander Solzhenitsyn, in his book *The Gulag Archipelago*, praised Berdyaev by name for his uncompromising stance under pressure from the Communists.) Berdyaev had a contentious relationship with the Orthodox Church of his youth, but he counted this denomination most faithful to foundational Christianity.

While granting Berdyaev honor, Slaatte assigned philosophical dishonor to the writings of the British "logical positivist," A. J. Ayer and his cohort, in *The Dogma of Immaculate Perception: A Critique of Positivistic Thought*. These thinkers insisted (without scientific testability) that the only meaningful statements were scientifically testable in principle. So claims such as "Adultery is evil," "God is good," and "Sunsets are beautiful" are meaningless, except as emotive expressions—essentially fancy ways of saying, "Adultery, Yech/Boo!" "and "God and sunsets, Ahh/Yay!" Slaatte identified himself as "a balanced religious existentialist with a both/and dialectic of paradox beneath the ethical either/or," and he concluded that "positivist thinkers lose sight of the social reference," failing "to see how the developments in science are historically conditioned by the social and cultural milieu that contribute to the paradigms by which scientists theorize in a given period."[41] In this, he was tracking with the aforementioned Thomas Kuhn's point about the subjectivity and communal nature of science itself.

Regarding Slaatte's chosen label as a "balanced religious existentialist," he wrote prolifically on the topic, with such published titles as *The Paradox of Existentialist Theology: The Dialectics of Faith-Subsumed Reason-in-Existence* (1971) and *Time and Its End: A Comparative Existential Interpretation* (1980). When asked to define "existentialism" at a honors program seminar (his topic being "The Existential Perspective in Religion"), he pointed to the problem that high school football coaches faced in recruitment: "Boys would rather watch the game from the stands than be out on the field. The existential perspective, however, holds that one must get into the arena of life rather than sit in its grandstand" (*Parthenon*, October 27, 1967).

As for his Wesleyan connections, Slaatte had been ordained as an elder in the Methodist church in 1943 and had pastored in the Detroit area for fifteen years. His doctorate was from United Methodist-affiliated Drew University, which houses the denomination's archives and one of its leading theological schools. A statue of early bishop Francis Asbury (the namesake for the Methodist college and seminary in Wilmore, Kentucky) stands on the Drew campus. In this tradition, Slaatte published *Fire in the Brand: An Introduction to the Creative Work and Theology of John Wesley*; *The Arminian Arm of Theology*; *The Theologies of John Fletcher, First Methodist Theologian, and his Precursor, James Arminius*; and *A Purview of Wesley's Theology*.

Slaatte's blend of Methodist theology and philosophy generated some fairly dense prose:

> The leading role was given to the Word-bearing and Word-personifying Son of the Eternal Playwright, who would convey to men of historical existence the meaning of the existence and its destiny . . . Religiously, Berdyaev's view of the Logos involves an eternity whose redemptive dynamic gives to time a special eschatological depth.[42]

His Methodist sermons were more accessible, full of illustrations:

> While Governor of Texas, Pat Neff went to the state penitentiary one time intent on pardoning an inmate whom he would select, many a prisoner assured the governor that he was innocent. Just as the Governor was about to leave he noticed a forlorn-looking man. "Were you wrongly convicted?" said the Governor. "No," said the prisoner. "I was guilty, and they really let me off light." He was the man the Governor chose to pardon.[43]

And again:

> After severe torture in a filthy prison in Burma, [Adoniram] Judson appealed to the king to allow him to preach the Gospel in the capital city. The king shrewdly replied: "I'm willing to have a dozen preachers go, but not you, Judson. People won't listen to your Gospel, but they will take note of those scarred hands of yours."[44]

In his sermons, Slaatte loved to quote a wide range of people—in "Living Under Pressure," from 1 John 5:4, 5 (Branch Rickey, Jackie Robinson, Carl Jung, Henry Emerson Fosdick, and George Matheson); in "Finding that Higher Happiness" from John 15:1–11 (Friedrich Nietzsche, E. Stanley Jones, Westbrook Pegler, Søren Kierkegaard, and [Susanna] Wesley); in "Growing Old Gracefully" from 2 Corinthians 4:16 (William Cullen Bryan, Ralph Waldo Emerson, Benjamin Disraeli, Lord Byron, James Garfield, Abraham Lincoln, Robert Browning, Thomas Eliot, and Theodore Roosevelt).[45]

His printed messages ran about two thousand words (under fifteen minutes), and so are typically characterized as "homilies" (improvisations on a passage) as distinct from "expository sermons," which are more concerned with unpacking the text, verse by verse, with grammatical-historical commentary as well as illustrations and applications. This latter form is ordinarily identified with evangelical preaching, as contrasted with the pulpit deliverances of "mainline" congregations. An expository sermon generally runs two or three times as long as a homily. Of course, there is substantial overlap between the two sorts, and ministers in both traditions study "homiletics" (a cognate of "homily"), but the differences are manifest.

Slaatte signaled his mainline orientation in other ways. In his sermon on "Developing the Art of Growing Up" (from 1 Corinthians 13:11—". . . put away childish things"), he wrote,

> I am reminded of a young man who took a stand for Christ in a
> revival of sorts. He was overjoyed by one thing and one thing only.
> He was on his way to heaven. But when the minister tried to en-
> courage him to accept a little responsibility around the church he
> would have none of that. He was an infant, pure and simple, and
> had not yet risen above a self-centered, childish view of salvation.[46]

Without naming Billy Graham, Slaatte seems to distance himself ("a
revival *of sorts*") from the crusade evangelism Graham was known for or
the dramatic work of God that shook little Asbury College in 1970, when
a regular chapel service ended up running around the clock for days. (An
account of the latter is dramatically recounted in Robert Coleman's *One
Divine Moment*.) Slaatte speaks of the convert's joy "in one thing only"—
his access to heaven—and of his "self-centered, childish view of salvation."
While, of course, there are those whose spiritual excitement of the moment
doesn't pan out (for the Parable of the Sower and Soils in Luke 8 teaches as
much), revival conversions (whether in tents, stadiums, civic auditoriums,
or the local church) are notable for their impact on the culture, a striking example being the Wesleyan revivals of the eighteenth century. And
it's been observed that when a man or woman "gets saved," they have to
backslide to have fellowship with the rest of the congregation. They're so
eager to share their new faith with the lost and to pitch in with the ministry that they turn off those who've settled into a more sedate Christianity.
Self-centered, they're not. And, of course, there are any number of church
members who've not identified with Christ through "a revival of sorts," and
who have proven to be less than responsive "when the minister tried to encourage [them] to accept a little responsibility around the church." In other
words, Slaatte played off a caricature here, projecting his dismay unevenly.

Furthermore, he had no use for the "penal substitutionary" view of
Christ's crucifixion, the view that people deserve death and hell for their
indifference and hostility to the life-giving rule of God, but that God, in his
mercy sent his son to die in their place so that they wouldn't have to pay
the penalty for their sin. In the classic translations, the cross was a means
of "propitiation"—appeasing the wrath of our creator who is affronted and
grieved by sin. This is a strong, repellant, even insulting doctrine—that
God would require of his son Jesus a blood sacrifice to cover our sins. Evangelicals are generally not averse to this doctrine, convinced that they read
it in the Bible.

Mainliners, such as Slaatte, are not as inclined to embrace it. Indeed, in his sermon, "Glorying in the Cross," he offers what's called the "moral demonstration" view of the Atonement (from "at-one-ment," referring to our reconciliation with God). As Slaatte puts it, "He [Jesus] performed his own teaching" (to pray for one's persecutors); "Not that he paid a price to the Father that he might forgive us but that he revealed the cost of the divinely expendable 'love that will not let me go'"; for "it realistically expresses and makes us conscious of the nature of sin"; and "It is the divine spark that transforms men, who will then want to reform society."[47]

In other words, Jesus' death on the cross was personally validational, instructional, and inspirational; it was not metaphysically and judicially effectual. To think otherwise is to put God and us in a very bad light—that we would be so reprehensible as to need someone to die for us and that God would be so reprehensible as to demand it of Jesus.

In 1968, for the Impact program, Slaatte wrote a piece on the "New Morality: Responsibility or Decay" in connection with sexologist Lester Kirkendall's appearance. (The remarks were reprinted in the April 5 *Parthenon*.) Sizing up Kirkendall's take on these matters, Slaate demonstrated, to his credit, his philosopher's analytical skills and his minister's heart:

> With pronounced respect for individuals and their circumstances, the "new morality" is precisely articulated by Joseph Fletcher as "situation ethics," a moral outlook which tries to avoid the extremes of codified conduct on the one hand, and normless relativism on the other . . . Unless consistently God-centered in every sense, what prevents self-giving Agape from being perverted by Eros, the self-gratifying love that ranges from sex to success, symbolized today by the vanishing virgin, the debauched businessman and the punk politician, who suspends virtue for vanity or mammon, who gives only to get . . . Does it want the fruits of sacrificial love perhaps, without adequate faith-fed "roots"? Does it want a quantitative horizontal relevance without a qualitative, vertical reference?

Slaatte's tenure at Marshall extended from 1965 to 1989, a season in which he exercised substantial influence, one in which he served a term on the board of the Campus Christian Center.

Incidentally, Slaatte's philosophy colleague, John Plott, a graduate of the University of Benares in India, was keen on Gandhi, with convictions that led him to assume conscientious objector status during World War II. He set his sights on writing a history of philosophy from a "third-world perspective" in order "to foster international understanding." As Marshall historian Charles Moffat put it, "Doctor Plott's sartorial and tonsorial eccentricity . . . contributed to his being regarded on the campus as something of a character."[48] He was, indeed, a character. As Slaatte recalls, Plott lost track of over four hundred library books he'd checked out and distributed to his students for reading. And then there was the time that Plott was late for breakfast at a philosophy conference, and Slaatte found him in his room standing on his head in Yoga fashion. He goes on to recall, "As a Christian ethically he was often active in 'the Friends,' the Quaker society. More-than-average as a metaphysician he was ecumenical in every sense of the word and always concerned about improving social issues that affect society in general."[49]

The "Casean" Louis Jennings

Louis B. Jennings was a fixture at Marshall for many years. He first joined the faculty in 1948, with a 1945 BD from Crozer Seminary and later earned the PhD from the University of Chicago (1964). Thus credentialed, he headed the newly-created Bible department till his retirement in 1979—over three decades of influence. In an introduction to *Bibliography of the Writings of Shirley Jackson Case*, he's described as a disciple of Case, as one who "is vigorously engaging in an eminently Casean type of activity as professor of Bible and religion in Marshall College . . . [and] director of religious activities on the Marshall campus—in itself a full-time function for one man."[50]

"Casean activity" is nicely indicated by this account, by Jennings, of the reception given one of his beloved professor's works, *Jesus: a New Biography*, "one of his most influential books."

> This work, incidentally, indicates to a high degree the kind of reaction that has characteristically been stimulated by his scholarly activities. Following its publication the story of protest to the view of Jesus therein given was swift in rising. Several Chicago papers carried interviews with prominent ministers and religious leaders in the vicinity. On the whole, these were decidedly and strongly opposed to the results of the study. But that in the main Professor Cases's conclusions are accepted today by men of a liberal viewpoint is well known.[51]

It's not surprising that Case's "biography" of Jesus prompted dismay. It psychologized Jesus, focusing on his interpretation of himself or growing personal convictions about his role, without coming down on whether or not these convictions were grounded in reality. Case also treated the Gospels as public relations documents, crafted to serve the purposes of those "creating" Christianity. Again, Case was big on projecting motives and short on sizing the text up for truth. Here's a small sampling of Shirley Case's art:

- The garish display of the miraculous, with which the several gospel writers overlaid the story of Jesus' life, answered admirably to the demands of the gentile mission field where Christianity was now struggling for recognition against rival faiths that claimed to be media of divine healing . . . A continuous series of marvelous deeds, such as are spread upon the pages of the gospels, finds no suitable place in the manner of life becoming a preacher of reform in Israel.

- Under these circumstances it is altogether improbable that Jesus had ever called himself the "Son of Man." [The Gospels record seventy-eight occurrences of Jesus' doing just this, for it was his favorite self-designation.]

- Jesus had no intention of elaborating a system of ethical precepts specifically designed either temporarily or permanently for the present world-order.[52] [So much for the Sermon on the Mount, including the Beatitudes.]

Of course, judging motives is a treacherous game, for the tables may soon be turned, with one's asking what drove Jennings to think he was above traditional Christianity and what drove Marshall, from President Smith on down, to hire an instructor whose aim was to undermine the "simple faith" of the region.

In due season, Jennings generated his own controversy, but Marshall historian Charles Moffat counted him a sterling asset:

> Jennings was a progeny of the liberal, yet prestigious, divinity college in the University of Chicago—a progressive school that emphasized the historical and critical examination of religion. Indeed, this was a form of "religious exploration" that had been virtually unknown in the local area. Jennings admits that he had "probably moved too rapidly in endeavoring to upgrade the work of the department." Several influential religious leaders in the community expressed grave concern about the alleged unorthodoxy of Jennings' teaching, and efforts were made to dismiss the young instructor. Jennings said that fortunately for him: "There was a show

of strength by the faculty and by certain members of the administration, who held firmly to the conviction that freedom of inquiry was a necessary prerequisite for an institution of higher learning." The college, accordingly, maintained its intellectual integrity . . . Dr. Jennings . . . was an exceptionally erudite scholar and a morally courageous, yet captious [faultfinding; difficult to please], member of the faculty; certainly, the Department of Bible has consistently reflected credit upon the institution.[53]

Of course, two matters are in play in Moffat's summary—academic freedom and the soundness of Jennings' teaching. The two items are separable, as is clear from the case of Henry Butz, professor of electrical engineering at Northwestern University. A Holocaust denier, he was excoriated by his department, his writings on the topic removed from Amazon, yet the university president said that Butz's tenure status protected his employment. While calling the writings on the Jews "odious," the president refused to move against him since his departmental work for the school was solid.

But Moffat goes beyond this, praising Jennings as "exceptionally erudite," one who "consistently reflected credit upon the institution." As for his critics, they were unhappy with only "alleged" unorthodoxy, discombobulated by a type of scholarship "virtually unknown in the area." One gets the image of agitated rustics naturally at odds with a new-fangled, shackle-free look at religion, a fresh perspective "guilty" only of exercising critical powers and giving history an honest look.

It's not clear that Moffat had a firm grasp on or devotion to "orthodoxy"; or that he understood the tenuous and demonstrably toxic presuppositions that these progressives brought to the table; or that he'd noticed their damage, manifested in the decline of denominations and institutions which imbibed in their perspective; or that he was familiar the depth and quality of scholarship to be found in evangelicalism. And never mind that West Virginia hill folk were being taxed to fund Jennings' efforts to disabuse their children of the "faith once for all delivered to the saints."

So we have a proudly non-evangelical scholar platformed at Marshall for decades. And it shows in his book, *The Function of Religion: An Introduction*. Therein, Jennings speaks of "a creative religion which can coordinate and direct toward life's fulfillment the varied concerns and interests which confront persons in life. The individual in society must be able to move forward within the framework of the cultural pattern."[54]

To get a fix on who's on board and who's not in this "creative" enterprise "moving forward within the culture," he speaks of the 1.

"Uncultivated Uncultured" folks who have discarded whatever religious faith they might have had and have rejected civilization, whether consciously or unconsciously; 2. "Uncultivated But Cultured," whose knowledge is superficial and who show no interest in digging deeper; 3. "Uncultured But Cultivated," who know a lot of things, but they don't engage the big questions of meaning and purpose; 4. "Cultivated and Cultured," those who've learned a lot and who've tied it all together in a progressive, coordinated program of life.

Jennings, of course, identifies with #4, and he proceeds to provide the ingredients for improving on ancient orthodoxy. As he explains,

> Religion has attempted to hold on to its traditional ideas, values, and forms simply on the basis of their historical authority. As its membership has been exposed to knowledge which has been produced by other disciplines, adherence to the faith has become difficult to maintain. Had there not been this obstinacy of the established faiths as they resisted this exposure to the enlarging thoughts and outlooks which were proceeding, the transition could possibly have been made easier and many of the old conflicts have been obviated. No religion worth its salt will be other than delighted to have every form of thoughtful examination carried out . . . Not only will religion encourage philosophy to explore its nature and character, it will also be responsive to the assessments. It will not be reluctant to reject some feature when it has been shown to be lacking in any genuinely tenable support. More importantly, it will incorporate whatever may have been projected as having value for a faith concerning man's relationship to the universe.[55]

He adds, "Religious experience . . . is the only legitimate place to begin. Even as metaphysics must start with the disclosures of empirical science, the same approach must be followed in religion."[56] It all sounds quite "enlightened," a word Jennings favors. ("Too many individuals have not been enlightened.") But what exactly is he talking about when he demeans "historical authority" and touts the "assessments of philosophy," "enlarging thoughts," and "the disclosures of empirical science"? Is he suggesting that Muslims abandon polygamy, practiced by their founder thirteen centuries ago, or that Christians abandon their opposition to it, following the teachings of their founder twenty centuries ago? Or, regarding polygamy, that science (divorce and abuse statistics?) or personal experience (whether it satisfies the individuals involved) should decide the question?

In a traditional, Christian-majority region (such as West Virginia), is he urging students to loosen their hold on the fourth-century Apostles Creed or the Reformation doctrine of *sola scriptura*? Does he reject the "analogy of faith," whereby the Bible is used to interpret the Bible, correcting mis-readings and undermining reliance on "lonely proof texts"? If not that, then how answerable is the Bible to science? If science says that a man three days dead in the grave doesn't come back to life, do we "modern" and "enlightened" folks toss out the Resurrection?

He goes on to counsel us that "organized religion fosters ignorance"; to disparage the "prevailing idea [which] is to keep the faith . . . [and to] not let it be disturbed by modern knowledge"; to assure us that "there can be no overt expression of religion which will be adequate for all persons" for "[W]e live in a much too high [sic] diversified universe for that sort of thing to be successful"; and to conclude, "The solution would seem to be that organized religion should serve as a reservoir or storehouse wherein there exists many and varied options which will serve as germinal seed for the production of individual and personal religious faiths."[57]

So the answer is religious pluralism, a theory diametrically opposed to the conviction of Marshall's founders—that Jesus is "the way, the truth, and the life" and that no one comes to God the Father or is saved except through Jesus (John 14:6; Acts 4:12). Still, it's one thing to grant the freedom to rank down the place of Jesus and quite another for the state to dun the citizens to install a pluralist to take the lead in religious training (or deprogramming) and in framing a public campus's religious affairs.

A November 15, 1962 letter from Andrew Bird, pastor of First Presbyterian Church, sheds light on the problem. Bird said he trusted President Smith to sort things out and praised him for his "excellent success in building up both the University and the Christian influence on campus." Nevertheless, he noted that "a good many of the more Bible centered churches had been somewhat distressed at the rather loose way in which the professor treated the meaning of revelation and the authority of scripture" but that they "had such confidence in you and your appreciation of the difficulties of this position in a state university that we had gone along gladly with this extreme liberal teacher because you felt it was necessary." Consequently, they "looked to Lander Beal and [their] denominational representatives rather than the professor of religion in relation to [their] students on the campus."

The Humanist Duncan Williams vs. "Trousered Apes"

In 1966, the English department brought an Oxford trained Welshman, Duncan Williams to campus, where he directed an interdisciplinary honors seminar in addition to his regular classroom duties. (His life experience included a stint in the Royal Marines and civil service work in East Africa.) During his tenure at Marshall (1966–1970), he wrote *Trousered Apes: Sick Literature in a Sick Society*, playing off an expression that C. S. Lewis coined in his seminal book, *The Abolition of Man*, denoting those who parade about in human garb while behaving like animals. (Incidentally, in the preface, Williams expressed appreciated for two Marshall department chairmen—Slaatte in philosophy and Brown in English.)

While Lewis was an apologist for the particularities of the Christian faith (through, for instance, *Mere Christianity*, the *Problem of Pain*, and *Miracles*), Williams dismissed proofs and defenses of the faith. Lewis embraced the "moral argument" (no moral law without a Lawgiver) and an "argument from longing/*Sehnsucht*" (no orientation toward things above unless there's an above). In contrast, in *Trousered Apes*, Williams wrote

> I have stated that theological considerations are secondary in this book, believing that an argument between an atheist and a believer resembles a dispute between two pygmies as to what lies on the other side of a 60-foot wall. The existence of God can neither be proved nor disproved and there always remains what Browning calls "The grand Perhaps".[58]

To be sure, Williams showed respect for the Christian tradition. He cited Philippians 4:8 ("Whatsoever things are true, whatsoever things are elevated, whatsoever things are just, whatsoever things are pure") and drew from Dante Alighieri, author of *The Divine Comedy*, to observe that man "in so far as he is rational . . . seeks for what is right—and in this he stands alone [above vegetable and animal], or is a partaker of the nature of the angels." Williams identified Dante as "a classical Christian humanist" (a status to which he himself aspired) and specified the ideal: "Western man, from pre-Socratic times, has recognized the essential dualism of his nature, but the combined forces of Christianity and classicism, utilizing what one may term moral absolutism, stressed the importance of the spiritual and frowned upon the sensual and animal."[59] On this model, Christ, Augustine, and Pascal, show up in the "canon" of civilization's thinkers and doers along with Homer, Shakespeare, Goethe, Buddha, Confucius, Socrates, Plato,

Galileo, Newton, and Pasteur—all of them assailed by the nihilistic, destructive ideology, which Williams identified with the murderous character Raskolnikov in Dostoevsky's *Crime and Punishment.*[60]

He cited the Scottish psychiatrist R. D. Laing as part of the problem for commending the hope that "all through school the young are provoked to question the Ten Commandments, the sanctity of revealed religion, the foundations of patriotism, the profit-motive, the two-party system, monogamy, the laws of incest and so on."[61]

While Williams paid some lip service to the importance of God consciousness, his big concern was the preservation and restoration of sanity and decency. He was a humanist very much concerned with the way that literature and the other arts were flowing with and hastening the decline of Western Civilization. He laid much of the blame on Romanticism, with its emphasis on emotions, and included, among the culprits, some Christians (William Blake, Søren Kierkegaard, and even John Wesley) and well as those less oriented on the traditional faith (William Wordsworth and John Keats). He lamented the way that the "classical temper" (marked by "security and satisfaction and patience") had been displaced by a spirit which was "insecure, unsatisfied, impatient." (Here he played off James Joyce's analysis.) Of course, the latter spirit marked the 1960s, and Williams was clearly not on board.

Williams didn't speak in generalities, but rather was very pointed in his critique, disparaging a wide range of offenders, including the writer Norman Mailer, the situational ethicist Joseph Fletcher, and the "yippie" agitator, Abbie Hoffman. And he was quite impatient with the conceits of modernism:

> To extol beauty, dignity and grandeur, both in man and nature, is not an escape from realism or from what is natural. There is nothing fundamentally more realistic or more 'natural' about a public urinal [referencing the "readymade" art of Marcel Duchamp], or a kitchen sink, or a paranoid-schizophrenic than there is about a tranquil lawn, or a cultivated household, or a balanced mind. All exist in the world, and a writer who concentrates exclusively upon the sordid and repellent aspects of life, implying that these are all, is as guilty of distortion as the authors of mawkishly sentimental novelettes.[62]

Malcolm Muggeridge, the British writer who'd turned to Christianity and conservativism from early enthusiasm for Communism and agnosticism, wrote, "*Trousered Apes* . . . is a cogently argued, highly intelligent and devastatingly effective anatomization of what passes for culture today, showing that it is nihilistic in purpose, ethically and spiritually vacuous, and Gadarene in destination."[63]

Melvin Miller and the Crusade Originals

As religious life at Marshall was taking a decidedly "mainline" turn, a seminal, contrasting figure appeared on campus in the person of Melvin Miller (in the 1968–1969 catalogue—"J. Melvin Miller, Assistant Professor Political Science, 1967. Ph.D. 1967, University of Rajasthan"). He'd worked for Campus Crusade for Christ, and right away, he started checking with churches in the area to get the names of students he might approach with plans for evangelistic outreach on campus. And sure enough, an original group formed up around him, heeding his call to "start a spiritual revolution"—Mike Hall, Tony Davis, Robin Crouch, and Jeanne Adkins (later becoming Jeanne Terry when she married Gregg Terry, introduced below).

Unlike the groups based in the Campus Christian Center, Crusade *per se* steered clear of social and political causes and focused on winning souls. They met in dorms, with well over a hundred students attending. Miller had a field-test copy of *The Four Spiritual Laws*, which students studied and shared from memory, in the firm expectation that they would present the gospel to at least fifteen students a week. When they gathered for dorm meetings (e.g., with over sixty in the freshman girls' dorm on Thursday night and another fifty students in West Hall), they sang with guitar accompaniment, conducted Bible studies, and heard the testimonies of the newly converted.

The impact was substantial, and many of the group's nucleus have gone on to full-time ministry in the years since. Though the Marshall Crusade chapter had no campus staff as such—just the shepherding of a faculty member—it had one of the largest in the nation by 1967–1968. For training, the leaders would make occasional trips to the University of Kentucky in Lexington, but they were essentially on their own. (The 1968 yearbook picture shows thirty-one Crusade members assembled.)

One of the early members was Gregg Terry, whom Miller won to the Lord using Crusade material. Gregg was zealous for the gospel, not at all afraid to share it broadly—and he soon got his chance, for in the fall of 1968, Cathy Buffalino, a member of the Marshall Students for a Democratic

Society (SDS) chapter, was engaged in a back-and-forth in *The Parthenon*, raising a number of points, to which Terry responded.

In a letter to *The Parthenon* (December 4, 1968), Terry addressed two claims Cathy had made. First, the SDS charged in their campus paper, the *Free Forum*, that a political science professor (Mel Miller) was requiring his students to do some community work through a government agency, and Gregg explained that this was just one option (and a good one, in that it meant "simply tutoring young Negro children once a week"). But the bulk of the letter addressed a second notion:

> The other point with which I feel compelled to take issue is unfortunately even more universally misunderstood, even by our society as a whole. Cathy's statement was "Jefferson was sincere, Samuel Adams was sincere, Dr. Martin Luther King Jr. was sincere, and Jesus Christ was sincere—and I am sure they all were 'sincerely unhappy,' sincerely frustrated, and sincerely confused."
>
> This time last year I would have, as I feel certain most people do today, agreed with this statement, particularly as it refers to this man Jesus. I too was unhappy, confused, and frustrated with the purpose and direction of my life. I was involved in numerous activities which we typically associate with a successful college life, including fraternity, student government, honoraries, dean's list, etc. Yet there was an indescribable void in my life. Then I met a group of students who seemed to have a new quality to their lives. They faced many of the same problems I did and most all of us as college students do, yet they had an uncanny ability to stay on top of problems, irrespective of circumstance. I asked them what was responsible for this quality in their lives and they said that it was Jesus Christ. They shared with me how He claimed to be God and how He claimed in Revelations [sic] 3:20, "I stand at the door of every man's heart and knock, if any man hears my voice and opens that door, I will come in to him."
>
> Obviously He was either lying or telling the truth. If He was lying, Christianity is no more than a pleasant fable, a myth. If however, by some far stretch of the imagination, He was telling the truth, it would be the most fantastic promise a man could ever be given. The only way I could ever know with certainty would be to apply the acid test and ask Him into my life on faith. If I was going to be consistent in life and intellectually honest, I was forced to test His word. The results have been phenomenal. I didn't see a burning bush or hear an audible voice from Heaven, but I have seen numerous changes occur in my life. I don't understand all the

theological implications involved, but this much I do know: Once I was unhappy, confused and frustrated; today, I have been set free from circumstance and my life has real purpose. I don't have any assurance that I won't encounter problems, in fact the problems I have faced recently have been worse than ever, but there is a new power in my life which is truly supernatural, enabling me to stay on top of problems. I don't have a magic wand to wave as I trod down a rosy path, but for the first time I have direction and meaning in my life. Sound fanatic? I would have thought so a year ago, but my life tells a different story.

No, Cathy, Jesus Christ was not unhappy, confused, or frustrated, but rather He offers the highest privilege and purpose life can offer, living moment by moment with Him, to every one who turns to Him. If you don't believe me, ask Him!

Graduating in 1969, Terry went on to study at St. Andrews in Scotland and Hebrew University in Jerusalem. Eventually, he earned the MDiv from Gordon-Conwell and the DMin from Reformed. He's now pastor emeritus of Huntington's Christ Community Church, having led the church from its founding in 1977 till 2017, when he retired.

Gregg became co-leader of Crusade with Mike Hall, whose father played on a late-1940s Marshall basketball team that finished high in the NAIA rankings. He was ordained and later was later elected to the West Virginia House of Delegates and the state senate, and in 2017 was appointed chief of staff to Governor Jim Justice.

Hall remembers Professor Miller as "unique to what happened." He was against the Vietnam War, was keen on racial integration, and an evangelical, manifesting a "combination of evangelism and social justice." As for the "social justice" angle, let's return to the campus SDS for a moment. Greg Terry's letter to *The Parthenon* had defended Miller from the group's Cathy Buffalino. But, in another context, Miller was attacked for defending their right to be on campus.

A little background: The SDS was an activist group of the New Left, begun in 1959 and passing from the scene in 1969. Their chief manifesto was Tom Hayden's *Port Huron Statement*, and their main causes were civil rights and opposition to the Vietnam War. Near the end, the group split into several factions, including the Weather Underground, of which Bill Ayers was a prominent member.

When the SDS pressed their cause for official campus recognition in early 1969, student senator Gregg Terry led the body to pass a resolution opposing this status. Though a 1965 poll showed Marshall student support for the Vietnam War running seven to one in favor of the conflict, by 1969, sentiment was more divided and vociferous. The SDS bid was a flashpoint both on campus and in Huntington. President Roland Nelson, with editorial support from *The Parthenon*, was for granting the permit. Many in the city were incensed by the prospect, and a big town-gown row erupted. Even Senator Robert Byrd pitched in, sending an anti-SDS letter to the local paper. Some local pastors—Dewey Parr of Highlawn Church of Christ and Paul Warren of Jefferson Avenue Baptist Church—were particularly energetic in rallying the troops to press President Nelson to desist. Indeed, the president was in hot water on a number of counts, one being his accommodation of Marxist historian Herb Aptheker on a recent Impact program, another being his brusque manner, strongly contrasting with that of his public-relations savvy predecessor, Stewart Smith. (After a two-year tenure, 1968–1970, Nelson left for a teaching position in North Carolina).

At the height of the conflict, the Campus Christian Center hosted a forum on the issue, with SDS petitioners on one side, the ministers on the other, and a "neutral" faculty panel, including Melvin Miller, in the middle. (By this time, Gregg Terry was queasy over the fulminations of some of his anti-SDS "allies" in the city.) At the meeting political science professor Keith Peters was hit with some jeers when he said that a college campus in a free society should be open to such divergent groups and opinions.

> [But] the strongest vilification was directed at political science instructor Mel Miller, whose comments enraged those opposed to recognition. Peters recalled that one man rose as Miller was speaking, pointed at him and said, "We know what you are. We know exactly what you are." I seemed to notice a sort of smile come over [Pastor] Warren's face. The opposition suspected Miller because of his alleged affiliation with the World Council of Churches, a liberal religious body that was one of the main targets of Mrs. E. Wyatt Payne's crusade against communism.[64]

Some real qualifiers here—"seemed," "sort of," "suspected," "alleged"— but enough to indicate that Miller was in the heart of two battles, to win souls to Christ and to shape social policy (whatever one might think of his choice of causes). Evangelism and public-policy interest weren't an either-or thing for Miller.

Back to evangelism: Miller struck up a strategic conversation with Hall as he did others, and he enlisted six of them to attend a Crusade event in Atlanta in December of 1967. (Miller paid Hall's way.) The original four plus Terry were joined by another from Baptist Temple in Huntington. These six became the core, who worked with Miller to start "College Life" meetings in the dorms and frat houses, to acquaint the campus with the "Four Spiritual Laws," and to speak publicly at the site of the campus clock. They even met on weekends, with prayer meetings in Ritter Park, and they were bolstered by a visit from Bob Prall, a Crusade representative from Chapel Hill, North Carolina, who spoke at the CCC on the relevance of Jesus for the twentieth century. (While there, he and his visiting team, provided the budding group with some leadership training.) At the forum, Prall said that a "quiet revolution is going on in college students turning to Christ," and then he fielded questions from Ashok Malhotra of *The Parthenon* (February 22, 1968):

Q: If Christ were alive today, would he participate in a civil rights or anti-war march?

A: I don't know. Christ himself told us there would be wars and rumors of wars. There are wars because man is trying to solve his own problems rather than letting God solve them The way to solve race and war problems is committing your life to Christ and having a love-faith relationship with God. The heart and core of the race problem are the individual attitudes of individual men towards one another. The attitude has to change. Millions of people have prejudices which have been changed to love by Christ.

Q: Is God dead?

A: Our concepts of God are dead, not God himself. No dead person can reveal his death. I know he is alive because today I see him changing lives.

Q: Would it be un-Christian if a person indulged in LSD and other drugs?

A: If a person attempts to fill the void by LSD or other drugs rather than Christ, the person is looking in the wrong direction. If primitive Christianity were used it could turn the world upside down. Primitive Christianity is a living personal relationship with Jesus Christ. It is not following a list of do's and don'ts but achieving a love relationship with God through Christ. The world needs love, individuals need love and only Christ can give love. As men's lives are changed by love possibly fewer wars will occur. As preventive medicine saves the lives of physically ill, love of Christ would save lives of those who are spiritually ill.

One of Melvin Miller's original four, Robin Crouch graduated in 1970 and went on to Campus Crusade headquarters in Arrowhead Springs, California, from where he traveled with Crusade founder, Bill Bright. He then served as Campus Crusade director at Ole Miss before returning to Marshall to lead her American Baptist work from 1984 to 1989. Indeed, in that latter post, he was over the entire American Baptist campus network (BCM) in West Virginia, a position from which he scheduled joint retreats involving his various groups.

He recalls that Ole Miss was a "have" school, Marshall a "have not" school. By this he meant that Marshall was then a "red-headed stepchild" in the West Virginia system since WVU had the law school, which produced a host of legislators who could favor their alma mater with funding. Be that as it may, both schools were quite open to his ministry. But Marshall was the standout, the most open of all state schools, with an amiable administration, providing access to their buildings. (Today, Crouch serves as adult ministry pastor at Huntington's New Baptist Church, where a 2017 newsletter reported that that fall's first weekly meeting of Cru at Marshall drew approximately one hundred eighty students "to hear the Gospel.")

Incidentally, looking toward November of 1970, Crouch recalls sharing a class in officiating with most of the seniors who died on the plane. Indeed, he knew about half of the seventy-five killed in the crash. He remembers in particular one of the unidentified victims buried in the common grave. This player "knew he needed to be a Christian, but there were things he wanted to do first." At least, this was his posture early in 1970.

Reflecting on the groups beginning, Mike Hall told *The Parthenon* (January 16, 1970):

> College Life was formed two years ago because it was discovered that students didn't have a balanced life. That is, the mind was being fed but the spiritual body was void . . . There were only four or five of us then, but we found students eager to learn about "experiencing" God in a personal way, so we began holding meetings every Thursday night.

That same year, the group grew to thirty and then to a weekly average of one hundred fifty in 1969. In the summer of 1969, twenty-four Marshall students attended Campus Crusade's Institute of Biblical Study at the headquarters in San Bernardino. Of the fifteen hundred students in attendance—from universities all across the land—Marshall had the largest contingent.

Back in 1967, during Miller's first year on the faculty, a "student liberal group" formed up on campus, connected nationally with the Unitar-
ian-Universalist Youth Movement, sponsored locally by the Huntington
Unitarian Fellowship. With officers from Huntington, Barboursville, and
Wheeling, they aimed to "serve as a campus voice for those students with
liberal views on political, social, or religious topics, and to provide stu-
dents an opportunity to discuss pressing issues of our time" (*Parthenon*,
December 13, 1967). As for such political and social discussions, the CCC
"Coffeehouse" had many of them already covered with a series of "Great
Decisions" programs slated for the 1968 school year—on, for instance, "The
Middle East," "Pills, Pot and Acid," "Police State Mentality," "The Psychology of Riots," and "American Power and Foreign Policy" (the latter led by
Melvin Miller). As for religion, the dramatic growth of Crusade Bible stud-
ies indicates that Trinitarian theology had greater appeal than its Unitarian
counterpart on campus.

8

November, 1970

THE CRASH OF SOUTHERN Airways flight 932 on November 14, 1970 was a stunning *catastrophe*. (The Greek root of this word signals an utter, downward turning.) But in the midst of this horrific season of loss, gratifying spiritual phenomena were in play.

Ernie Wilson Comes to Campus

As 1970 came around, Alan Wild was a "crazy, bar-hopping, pot-smoking" young man, angry at the Vietnam war.[65] Though he attended a Presbyterian church, he was, by his own admission, spiritually lost. In this state, he was confronted by a man who challenged him to be "really real," to "just become a Christian," and to come to Bible study and meet with some believers he'd not yet met. He started reading about becoming "born again," and "a peace came over him."

Wild attended a local meeting where Billy Graham associate, Ross Rhoads from Valley Forge, Pennsylvania, spoke, and he liked him. Before long, Alan was returning to his old bars, but this time to witness. He was impressed by Billy Graham's book, *Jesus Generation*, and his parents, who'd been anxious over his old life, were relieved to see their son transformed. As Wild recalls, four or five accepted Christ as a result of his evangelism, some of them at First Presbyterian Church.

When classes at Marshall got underway in the fall, he continued his gospel work on campus and joined others in inviting Ernie Wilson, a black evangelist from Philadelphia, to speak at the Campus Christian Center. The turnout was good. Wilson was fifty-nine at the time, the son of a Jamaican who was converted in Panama while working on the canal. The family became active in church, but it was not until they moved to New York when Ernie was in his late teens that he became a Christian.

Before that, he was something of a rebel, with his interests running more to jazz and boxing. He played saxophone in a number of groups and would often come home after 2:00 a.m., when the clubs closed. His anxious mother would often ask, "Ernest, when will you accept Christ as Savior?" and he'd say he would get around to it in due time. But one day in particular, things didn't look promising. His bandmates were coming to pick him up for a move to Hollywood (tantamount, in his case, to running away from home). Not aware of his impending departure, his mother once again pressed the gospel on him, this time with tears. Affected by this show of emotion, he agreed to follow her into his father's study so that he might pray for him. Responding to Romans 10:13, he began to "call upon the name of the Lord," and, instantly, by his account, the Holy Spirit pierced his head like an arrow, travelled down through his body, and exited his feet. When he rose from his knees, he'd been saved.

He was a changed man, eager to rise for 5:30 prayer meetings and preparing for a lifetime of ministry, service lasting more than six decades. In those days, Billy Graham was coming to prominence as a preacher and vice president of Youth For Christ. Since blacks were not part of that movement, Ernie started Christ for Youth in Philadelphia, and the two groups began to work together. Then, while he was pastoring for thirteen years in that city, he founded Manna Bible Institute, and, in due course, he pursued his own studies at Philadelphia Bible Institute (later Philadelphia College of the Bible) and Reformed Episcopal Seminary. (Years later, Princeton Seminary would give him an honorary doctorate.) Though his base was in Philadelphia, he ended up traversing the world as an evangelist, going as far as India with the Billy Graham Evangelistic Association.

In an interview stored in Wheaton College's Billy Graham Center archives, he gave a glimpse of his pastoral and prophetic perspective. Recalling his childhood days at the Christian Mission of Panama, where they "sang happily" and "preached fundamentally," he spoke of their moral standards, whereby members could be put out of the fellowship and denied access to the Lord's Supper if they fell into sin, whether through strong drink, prostitution, or gambling. (Indeed, children of the church were reprimanded if they played marbles for keeps.) Only by coming before the church and publicly repenting could they be restored.

Lamenting the loss of concern over holiness in the contemporary church, he observed that God's people had grown cold, that life in the Spirit was a thing of the past, and that consciences were callous. He spoke, for example, of how Philadelphia parishioners would attend the morning service and then head to Atlantic City to gamble on Sunday afternoon. He spoke too of the generosity of that early Panamanian church, wherein men with several suits would give one to a member who had only one. Today, in contrast, someone would drive a new car to church but never think to give a ride to one without a car.[66]

"Governor" Brown's Last Week

With such pointed observations, Ernie Wilson held the Marshall students spellbound. Some of them were football players sitting on the front row at that Campus Christian Center gathering, and, at the "altar call," at least one of them, "Governor" Brown, responded. Little did he and the other players know that several days later, on the upcoming weekend, they would perish in a plane crash.

That fall, Brown had been a mainstay of the defense, credited, for instance, with a critical tackle on a goal line stand in the season's opener, a victory over archrival Moorhead State. (Incidentally, seventeen years later, his son Delongelo, played defensive back for Marshall, having considered signing with Liberty.)

Perhaps Brown's response to Ernie Wilson's message that week help fortify him for a role he would play not long before boarding the bus for the airport on Friday. As Craig Greenlee recounts in his book, *November Ever After*, a fight broke out after an intramural football game between the Black United Students and the all-white Kappa Alpha fraternity. Tensions were high throughout the game, in part due to the perception that calls were slanted in KA's favor, and, then, things exploded when some KA pledges ran across the field with a Confederate flag. The fight lasted about forty-five minutes, and some were rushed to the hospital. Soon thereafter, another disturbance broke out in the cafeteria and then moved to a dorm lobby, with around one hundred fifty students, black and white, primed for a fight.

> One of the first players to enter the crammed lobby was "The Governor." At five feet, nine inches and 230 pounds, he wasn't among the biggest who played on the line. But he certainly had a knack for carrying a conversation in a soothing manner. In this instance, his

presence produced an air of calmness in the face of an imminently explosive situation. He was one of the *cooler heads*.

This natty dresser from Atlanta, Georgia, usually sported a stylish brim. He had a way of relating to everybody regardless of skin color or culture. It's hard to imagine anyone not liking him. Had he lived, it would not have surprised me if Gov would have carved out a nice career niche in the political arena.

At this moment, though, Larry Brown's persuasive skills were desperately needed. There wasn't much time for him to do very much. But in the few minutes he had, Gov managed to get his point across, which helped to avert what could have been a frightening chain of events. In a jam-packed lobby, I wasn't close enough to Gov to hear what he said. Whatever it was, people listened. And they responded by backing off from confrontation and allowing their anger to subside.

Bill Redd was close enough to hear what Gov had to say. He told me, "I remember Governor jumping in the middle (of the crowd) and saying, "Break this stuff up!" He pretty much let everybody know that the first blow thrown would have to come though him. He ordered everybody to break it up and go home."

The police did their part to quell the disturbance, but they certainly got a little help courtesy of Larry Brown.

After Gov arrived at the scene, other players filed though the area, curious about what was going on. They couldn't hang around for too long; they had an airport-bound bus to catch.[67]

Flight 932

The tragic event that followed on November 14 is well chronicled, particularly in the coverage of Huntington's *Herald-Dispatch*, which published compilations of their news reports on the fiery crash and its immediate aftermath.[68] The fateful night is typically spoken of in terms the loss suffered by the football team, and, indeed, thirty-seven players—all who were on board—perished, but there were thirty-eight others on the plane, including twelve on the coaching/athletic/university staff, five on the aircraft crew, and twenty-one from the community, including four physicians, three of whom were accompanied by their wives; a city councilman; a delegate elect to the state legislature; an industrialist; and three who'd been alumni or booster club presidents—this in a town of seventy-three thousand, with a university of thirty-five hundred. It led a nurse at Huntington Hospital to lament, "This town died today."

The ill-fated Southern Airways DC-9 was a chartered jet, whose expense was defrayed in part by the boosters who joined in the flight. (At 1970 prices, the $50 ticket covered round trip air, a night's lodging, a meal, and admission to the football game.)

The game itself—a 17–14 loss to the East Carolina Pirates—was disappointing, particularly since a questionable, intentional-grounding call ruined a promising, last-minute drive. But there were some outstanding performances, including one by the aforementioned Larry "Governor" Brown, who was in on eighteen tackles, seven of them unassisted.

Doctors in Gullickson and Prayerful Songs in the CCC

The Huntington *Herald-Dispatch and Advertiser* ran a Jack Seamonds story on the disaster the morning of the 15th—"Sobs, Anguish Pierce Cold, Rainy Night at Marshall University." As one observed, "The first thing that hit you, that brought the story home, was the cries of those being treated by doctors for shock. Mattresses were lined up on the floor in Gullickson Hall [the athletic building]." Meanwhile, a gathering was underway in the Campus Christian Center, with seven Marshall campus ministers and four hundred students in attendance. (This event was pictured briefly in the movie, *We Are Marshall*, set in the actual building.)

They sang *Kumbaya* ("Someone's hurting, Lord . . .") and "no one dared not sing." Then the prayers came: "They, those who have been so dear to us, have so soon passed by. He is watching us. He is here with us. And the Lord shall watch over them as they enter the Kingdom of Heaven." There were Amens as well as the sound of a siren passing on 5th Avenue.

"Doc" Eshelman's Visit

Upon hearing of the crash, Dr. Ira "Doc" Eshelman, chaplain of the New Orleans Saints, booked the first flight he could to Huntington. As the first team chaplain in the NFL, he worked without a salary: "My payment is seeing a football player achieve a new feeling of inner faith." He said that his hardest task up till the Huntington trip was helping players whose careers were ended by injury. But, he added, "It will never be quite as difficult now that I've been to Marshall. Because the football players here have not only lost their careers; they've lost their lives."

Over his eighty-eight years, Eshelman had a fruitful ministry in both church and parachurch contexts, but his work for the NFL was most remarkable. For one thing, he began the practice of leading pre-game chapels for the players, an institution that spread to every team in the league. A graduate of Moody Bible Institute, he stayed true to his evangelical faith, and memorial gifts were directed toward Campus Crusade's Jesus Film Project, among other causes.

For reference, Eshelman's trip to Marshall came the weekend after New Orleans Saint place kicker Tom Dempsey broke the NFL record with a 63-yard field goal (wearing a special shoe because he was born without toes on his kicking foot), a record it took twenty-eight years to tie and forty-three years to break.

A Voice at 3:00 A.M. and a Mother's Premonition

Phil Wilks, who both played and student-coached at Marshall, was a close friend of Roger Childers, one of the players who died in the crash. Having been injured back in 1967, Phil was asked to coach the freshman team in 1968, and Roger was one of his players before becoming a varsity starter at linebacker his sophomore year. Then, in turn, Roger was sidelined, he by a brain tumor requiring surgery, and, for a span, he traveled with the team as a manager. Through it all, he and Phil maintained a warm relationship, one that deepened after Phil's graduation in the spring of 1970. He'd hired Roger to do some construction for him that summer, and he'd "be at the house all the time." On into the fall, Roger asked him to be in his wedding, scheduled for the week after Marshall's last game at Ohio University. Of course, that was not to be, and neither was the fulfillment of Roger's farewell words to Phil as he prepared for the East Carolina trip, "See you when I get back."

Wilks heard the news of the crash on the radio and drove to the Rogers house to ask his parents if his friend had been on the plane. Later, in bed in his cinder-block apartment, with his bedroom illuminated by the glow of streetlights in the alley, Phil was awakened at 3:00 a.m. by a voice that sounded like Roger's, saying, "Phil, I'm okay." It made him sit straight up in bed.

At the time, as Phil recalls, he was not strong in the faith, and the season of mourning was very difficult for him, an anxious time. Though he served as a pall bearer at Roger's funeral, he stayed away from the other events.[69]

Sunday Morning Church

Kris Wilks, with a bachelors and masters from Marshall, as well as other university studies in support of her health education work in Louisville, belongs to a distinguished football family at Marshall (including the aforementioned Phil).[70] She recalls that at church the next day, there was "a numbness, a silence that couldn't be explained." The town was, indeed, stunned, for there were so many overlapping connections. For instance, her brother Phil was married to Pam Slaughter, a Marshall cheerleader who had cheered with and mentored the Chambers girls, who lost their parents in the crash.

Kris traces her family's strength for those days back to the ministry of her grandfather, a Methodist minister who died in 1971: "That's how we all got through it. That was our family culture. Mom and Dad modeled it."

Andrew Earles, digital media specialist with Marshall's special collections department, recalls that not everyone had watched the late night news on Saturday, so they were hit with the report in the Sunday morning paper. At that point, "the town went into shock." It was a particularly poignant time, just two weeks before Thanksgiving, and, at church, talk and prayers turned to the needs of the children of those who died, and to their own children—"Hug your kids; you or they could be gone in a blink of the eye."[71]

That same Sunday morning, Teddy Shoebridge's mother Yolanda went to church in his Lyndhurst, New Jersey, hometown. The priest thanked her for showing people she didn't hate God. Her reflection, when interviewed in 1999: "I don't. If you look and search, you see God is not a mean person."

Bos and Dotty Johnson also have vivid memories of that Sunday and the days after the crash. He was news director and anchor at WSAZ at the time (retiring in 1976 after twenty-five years at the station, after which he assumed a teaching role in broadcast journalism at Marshall), and his news casting appears in the documentary, *From Ashes to Glory*. She was a prof at Marshall at the time. Interviewed together about a month before Bos's death in 2014, and with the assistance of daughter Susan, they recalled the sad sight of a girl walking down the church aisle the morning of the 15th, uttering in total denial, "No, my parents weren't on that plane." Then, the following Wednesday, Dotty walked into her 9:00 class and was able to offer spiritual counseling: "Talk about an opportunity for Christian witness."[72]

The Memorial Services and the Funerals

The day after the crash, a 1:30 service was held in Huntington's Veterans Memorial Field House, with seven thousand in attendance.

> The Rev. Robert D. Cook, rector of St. John's Episcopal Church, set the tone for the memorial in his invocation which found as its theme a sorrow measured by the compassion of God, in whose keeping was commended the departed. The mourning community was asked to walk in trust. When the Rev Chas H. Smith, pastor of First Baptist Church, read from Ecclesiastes the familiar, "for everything there's a season," there was visible weeping . . . Mrs. Jane Shepherd, professor of music, sang "The Lord's Prayer" and a university chorus directed by Dr. Paul A. Balshaw, led the singing of "O God our Help in Ages Past."

Ministers were not the only ones to bring a message from the Word of God. As reported in *The Parthenon* (November 18, 1970), acting president, Donald N. Dedmon (who went on lead Virginia's Radford University to new heights, 1972–1995), began his remarks by reading Psalm 24 ("The earth is the Lord's and the fulness thereof . . . Lift up your heads, O ye gates . . . and the King of glory shall come in . . ."). In his remarks, he maintained that "belief in God and in immortality . . . gives us the moral strength and the ethical guidance we need for virtually every action in our daily lives." Along the way, he quoted Wernher von Braun's "Why I Believe in Immortality" and observed, "Science has found that nothing can disappear without a trace. Nature does not know extinction. All it knows is transformation!" His point was that the victims of the crash lived on in the hands of "the Lord of hosts," "the King of glory."

Thus they began to say good-bye to the seventy-five who had died, a service to be followed by many services. C. E. Wilson, later an elder at Christ Community Church (and extra in the movie, *We Are Marshall*), lost some close friends—Mike Blake in particular—and he recalls attending six or seven funerals in the days after the crash.[73] And some found themselves on lengthy road trips: In the Winter 2000 edition of *Marshall* magazine (in a reprint from the *Chicago Tribune*, September 5, 1999), Julia Keller remembers how her father, a math professor, got involved:

> With so many funerals happening simultaneously, Marshall's stunned athletic department was having a difficult time finding enough university representatives to attend them all. My father volunteered to give the eulogy at the funeral of Scottie Lee Reese,

a 19-year-old linebacker from Waco, Texas. So my parents loaded Cathy, Lisa and me into our family's blue and white Volkswagen bus and took off for Waco, an approximately 1,000-mile drive from southwestern West Virginia. Scottie's funeral was held a week after the crash at the Tolliver Chapel Missionary Baptist Church.

(Scottie's mother, Jimi, reported years later, that her faith remained "a railing she can grasp when she feels as if she might be falling." She observed, "I was brought up not to say, 'Why him?' My mother said, 'He was only loaned to you. The Lord wants him back.' Never question what the Lord does.")

The November 18 issue of the *Herald-Advertiser* began to announce the funeral arrangements, all with Christian church connections, some local, others dotted across the country. There were substantial delays in other arrangements because of the horrific nature of the crash, so catastrophic that, by the evening of the 16th, only fifteen of the seventy-five bodies had been identified: Athletic Director, **Charles Kautz** (St. John's Episcopal); **Dr. Ray and Shirley Ann Hagley** (Highlawn Baptist); **Mike Prestera** (Our Lady of Fatima Catholic); **Murrill Ralsten** (Johnson Memorial Methodist); **Gary George** (Piney View Bible); Offensive Coach, **Jim "Shorty" Moss** (Highlawn Baptist); **Dr. Joseph and Margaret Chambers** (Highlawn Presbyterian); **Dr. G. H. and Phyllis Preston** (St. John's Episcopal); Junior LB **Willie Bluford** (Zion Hill Baptist); **E. O. and Alaine Lois Heath** (Trinity Episcopal); **Gene Morehouse** (St. Joseph's Catholic); Junior WR **Dennis Blevins** (Sacred Heart Catholic); Manager **Roger Childers** (Highlawn Baptist); **Dr. H. D. and Courtney Proctor** (Enslaw Park Presbyterian); **Al Carelli** (Our Lady of Grace Catholic); **Dr. Brian O'Connor** (Trinity Episcopal); Junior QB **Ted Shoebridge** (Sacred Heart Catholic); Junior OG **Tom Howard** (New Haven Methodist); Senior C **Richard Dardinger** (Grace Lutheran); **Arthur Harris Sr. and Jr,** the latter a Sophomore RB (First Methodist, Passaic, NJ); Sophomore LB **Mike Blake** (Highview Methodist).

Additionally, on the 16th, a memorial service was held at Huntington First Baptist Church, where ten of the players were members—Dennis Blevins; Larry Brown; Robert Van Horn; Freddy Wilson; Willy Bluford; Larry Sanders; Bobby Hill; Joe Hood; Art Harris; Scott Reese. And then another at St. Mary's Hospital. (That same evening, a televised moment of silence was observed before the NFL's Monday Night Football game between the Dallas Cowboys and the St. Louis Cardinals.)

At Fairfield Stadium the next Saturday, at 1:30, when kickoff was originally scheduled for play with the Ohio University Bobcats in Athens, another observance began, this involving a wreath placed at midfield. For this occasion, Paulist priest and team chaplain, Robert Scott led in prayer. (In the fall of 1970, Scott had begun his ministry as the Catholic priest at Marshall, having served previously at St. John's, Ohio State, and West Virginia, where he was chaplain to the football team.) He intoned

> O Lord, of all of us, you know how human we all are, and thus you do understand why we must be here at this very hour. We know that there will be no game today. The game has been called off by your summons of our friends to yourself. But we are human and selfish, and we must cry over their absence. So we have come to their home field. To show our affection for them, we lay a wreath. Perhaps, as we stand together on this turf, where they gave their all for us, we may feel a little bit closer to them, our brothers.

"I Guess God Was With Him"

Wes Hickman, a center, was dropped from the trip roster on Thursday, the day before the outgoing flight. When contacted by the press, his mother, Mrs. Roy Hickman of Overland Park, Kansas, said, "I have shed many a tear for the other boys," and, regarding her son, "I guess God was with him."

Of course, the sovereign God was with all of the crash victims, and it would be unjust to suggest that those who died were, therefore, less connected with God. But it is fair to consider what purposes God had in allowing the death of some, but not of others. What purpose might there have been for the varying outcomes? Over a dozen cases press this question upon us.

Because of sprained ankle suffered three weeks prior to the flight, **Felix Jordan** was cut at the last minute from the trip, with his being pulled off the bus to his dismay; **Gregory Finn** missed the trip because of a knee injury (this being his third close-brush with death, having already survived two serious car accidents); **Rick Taglang** simply arrived late and missed the plane; **Ed Carter** had gone home for his father's funeral in Pampa, Texas; **John Calvin** had been off the travel squad for several weeks; equipment manager **John Hagan** drove the truck with all the gear to and from the game, having refused to fly out with the team ("I'm superstitious about Friday the 13th. Something just told me not to go on this trip"); though the coach asked the chaplain, the **Rev. Robert Scott**, to accompany them on the trip and join them on the sidelines during the game, he declined because it would take him away from the regular Saturday night mass; Assistant Coach **Red Dawson** drove to and from the game on a recruiting trip; Assistant Freshman Coach **Gail Parker** flew down with the team, but rode back with Dawson (He'd switched places with kicking coach Deke Brackett, who'd driven down with Dawson); **Frank James**, a linebacker and defensive end, had made an earlier trip but missed this one because of a hand injury; defensive end, **Pete Naputano** and tackle **David Withers** were both sidelined by injuries and spent the weekend in Altoona, Pennsylvania; **Nate Ruffin** was sidelined by calcium buildups on one of his arms, so troublesome that he had been playing with it supported by a sling; freshman **Kevin Jones**, an equipment manager, who'd been scheduled for the trip but called away to his grandmother's funeral.

A more remote instance concerns retired Florida State coach, **Bobby Bowden**. The year before, he'd been offered the coaching job at Marshall. At the time, Bowden was an assistant at West Virginia, and he chose, instead, to take the head coach position in Morgantown. He recalls that on November 14, 1970, WVU had upset a visiting Syracuse team, and, as was the Bowden custom after every home game, they hosted an evening gathering of administrators, staff, and fans in his home, a group that typically included the university president as well as the athletic director and coaches.

They were stunned when, over the TV, they got news of the crash in Huntington. He thought immediately of Red Dawson, whom he had coached as an assistant at Florida State in the mid-sixties. He expected to see Red's name among the victims as they were posted on the televised report, but was relieved to see it missing. He says Red was "a favorite, fun to be around," and, through the years since 1970, they've stayed in contact.[74]

Had Bowden been on that plane, he would have left a wife and six children (two girls and four sons), and the legacy portrayed in the documentary, *The Bowden Dynasty: A Story of Family, Faith, and Football*, would not have materialized.

And, of course, a number of players have spoken of the role faith played in sorting out their survival. For instance, Kevin Jones recounts his eventual release from a sense of guilt over missing the flight. He'd been troubled by the question of why he'd been spared. But then he found help in church, where, with his two sons, he heard two other survivors speak— Nate Ruffin and Ed Carter. It was then and there that a friend suggested his purpose was "to be a husband, a father, a brother, a son (who helps take care of his father who is in a nursing home, and mother who lives alone), a friend to those who need help." By Jones's account, "I found myself saying yes to things I never imagined myself doing."[75]

Then there is Ed Carter, whose journey led him into the ministry. In 2014, he explained this development in an FCA-connected talk at Bethune-Cookman University, a school where his 1971 teammate Jim Pry was serving as offensive coordinator. As reported by that Daytona Beach school,

> Ed Carter escaped death that day, but the former Thundering Herd standout considers March 10, 1974 as the most important day of his life. Carter acknowledges that day as the one he accepted Jesus Christ as his Lord and Savior. Since then, he has traveled as an evangelist, preaching the Gospel and making the most of each and every day of a life he firmly believes was spared for this reason. "There was a plan for me," Carter said when he addressed the Bethune-Cookman football team this past Tuesday night. "God has watched over me. I turned my life over to him that night in 1974. If I hadn't, I'd be dead or in an institution right now" he told over 100 student-athletes, coaches and administrators . . . Carter had a brief fling with the pros, earning an offer to the Buffalo Bills training camp, but a hamstring injury impeded his progress. He entered the workforce, first at a steel mill and then as a teacher. He earned his degree in 1974, but he had the feeling that his life wasn't complete. It became complete that night in March. "God told me I was a sinner," Carter said. "Right then and there, I accepted."[76]

Talk of God

We've taken a brief look at remarks, prayers, and hymns included in those early services, but much else was being said with reference to God—his revelation and his ways. For instance, the Emmy winning video (Outstanding Sports Documentary), *Ashes to Glory*,[77] reveals the following statements, offered in those dark November days, and later as the team and community witnessed a dramatic comeback:

- a Holiday Inn sign with the words, "The Lord Giveth, The Lord Taketh Away"

- West Virginian Governor Arch Moore's observation, "As a governor, these are acts of God. And where he picks to undertake to deliver his message, for whatever reason it may be, I don't know."

- and later, reflecting on the first game played by the reconstituted team, former player David Walsh's recollection, "I think we all realized there were some people watching us, pulling for us, from a different vantage point, you know; they had good seats."

- at that same time, Nate Ruffin's use of the language of Genesis 2 (where Adam first saw Eve), to describe the "Young Thundering Herd" who'd taken the field: "Bone of my bones. Flesh of my flesh. They've come to life."

Et Cetera Foreshadowing

Ironically, or perhaps poignantly, in the Spring 1970 issue of *Et Cetera*, we find two pieces that touched on death. One is a short fable by Joseph A. Seward, "Bridge on the River Styx," which draws on Greek mythology to talk about crossing from this world to the underworld. Seward salts his tale with references to certain faith groups ("Protestant Reformed and Catholic Orthodox") but the piece is cryptic. The second is a poem by Richard Napier, "When my Life is Done."

> Bury me beneath the weeping willow
> Where the flimsy branches softly billow
> In the whisperi'ng [sic], vagrant wind.
> When dawdling days of darkness descend.
>
> Bury me where the first spring
> Buds brave the winter's cling.
> Let me lie in the warm spring sun
> And rest—when my life is done.

Sunshine on Loan

In his book, *A Coach in Progress*, Red Dawson recalls the drive he made back to Huntington once he'd heard the bad news in route.[78] As he passed the hours with fellow coach Gail Parker, he repeatedly mouthed the lyrics from Hank Williams' song, "Funeral":

> . . . On the altar was a casket and in the casket was a child . . .
> Then rose a sad, old colored preacher from his little wooden desk . . .

And he said, "Now don't be weepin' for this pretty bit of clay
For the little boy who lived there has done gone and run away
He was doing very finely and he 'ppreciates your love
But his sho nough father wanted him in the big house up above

The Lord didn't give you that baby, by no hundred thousand miles
He just think you need some sunshine and he lent it for a while
And he let you keep and love him 'til your hearts were bigger grown
And these silver tears you're shedding now, are just interest on the loan . . .

And so my poor dear mourners, let your hearts with Jesus rest
And don't go to criticiz'n' the one what knows the best
He has given us many comforts He's got the right to take away
To the Lord be praised in glory, now and ever, let us pray

Throughout the books and clippings, we find no record of skeptics' declaring that the disaster was evidence that there was no God, or that the Lord was malevolent or indifferent. Rather, reverent God-consciousness was everywhere to be found, though often expressed as sad puzzlement, the sort heard from a "red-eyed coed" who stepped out from the Campus Christian Center into that cold, rainy, Saturday night: "God, what has happened? What has happened?"

9

The Following Year

As NOTED IN THE preface, the tragedy touched the souls of those who remained, and the ripples continued on throughout 1971.

A Knock on the Door

Baptist Student Union (SBC) director Dwain Gregory recounts an incident occurring on the Sunday evening before classes resumed in January. (He'd come to Marshall in the fall of 1969, as the first SBC/BSU man, and served for three years. The crash occurred thirteen months after his arrival.) Around 10:00, he answered a knock on the door at the BSU house at 1670 Sixth Avenue and discovered a group of students he didn't know wanting to talk with him. Right off, one said, "Somebody told us you were the Jesus guy. We're not Christians, but we want to be. Is this where we come to be saved?"[79]—a student minister's dream. He welcomed them in, explained the gospel, and, sure enough, some were ready to receive Christ as their Savior and Lord.

Dwain adds that this was not an isolated incident, but rather the outworking of a heightened spiritual sensitivity that marked the campus throughout the spring. The crash had brought on a lot of soul searching and concern over eternal destinies should life on earth be cut short. Consequently, attendance at his meetings and the meetings of other campus groups was strong, and response in terms of conversions and rededications was unusually high.

This is not to say that the campus paper, *The Parthenon*, was full of stories on the religious impact of the crash, but this might well be a

reflection of the editors' obliviousness or indifference toward such matters. Still, there was some notice of religious affairs. Indeed, the paper gave
Gregory a voice, with a photo, in the March 18, 1971 issue—"'Revolution'
replaces 'tradition.'"

Gregory told the writer, Sharon Harless, that his group was part of a
"Revolution for Christ," intent on leading students to know and grow in the
Lord. In this connection,

> Students are going to hear more about Christ this semester than
> ever before . . . [and] speak for Christ. The traditional "hush" at-
> mosphere about Christ is being placed aside. Fans cheer for their
> team. Christians can cheer for their Christ. Christians are taking
> a different attitude about Christ. Christ is known as the greatest
> Revolutionist and the BSU is joining the "Revolution for Christ."
> They want to make people think and to let them know that Christ
> is the answer . . .
>
> Students are seeking and asking to know more about Christ
> now . . . Students are beginning to ask "Why?" "Who am I?" "Why
> am I here?" and "Where do I go?". . . The answers to these ques-
> tions can be found through Christ.

To foster this search and growth, BSU met Tuesday and Friday nights
at 7:00, and a variety of "Bible study groups, prayer groups, and share
groups (where students talk about whatever they wish) also met at the
house, which was open 24/7 so that any time a student has a problem or
just wants to talk, he can come." (The 1970 yearbook offers a group shot
of seventeen BSU members, with the names of five not pictured. The 1971
yearbook shows twenty-seven, with no mention of those not present for
the photo.)

Furthermore, they'd formed a quartet (with Gregory, sophomores
Nancy Williamson and Mike Rice, and freshman Ray Jones). The group
formed on a mission trip to Philadelphia "ghettoes" in the summer of 1970,
was now singing in coffee houses, and was planning "sing-ins" on campus.
The BSU also anticipated "share groups on the campus lawn," a banquet in
April, and a "Rally for Christ."

Much of this sounds like standard evangelical outreach, but it had an
unmistakable, 1970s, counter-culture tone. As Harless put it, "The reason
for this sudden action now, Gregory feels, is that students are breaking away
from the establishment now. They are tired of the impersonal-type society."

In a series of conversations, Gregory unpacked his story, including
these items:

- After the initial meeting with inquiring students the night of January 3, 1971, at least one student a day (sometimes two or three) came up for Christian counsel (often evangelistic inquiry) until the third week in March, when spring break occurred. And Roman Catholic students were regulars at BSU.

- One of the students who received Christ was named Jimmy. He had hair down to his shoulders and would frequent a bar called The Library across the street, telling his parents he was "working late at the library." Someone brought him to Dwain for the gospel, a presentation to which he responded, and then Dwain would take Jimmy with him as he traveled around, having him give his colorful testimony: "I was so bad and feeling so bad I had to flush the [excrement] all down." The last Dwain heard, Jimmy was working with high school kids in a church.

- Some of the church people were not that enthusiastic about raised hands in worship, but there was general happiness over what was happening. The BSU had around thirty-five people to be baptized. Dwain came to his church, Westmoreland Baptist, and asked that they be baptized there. (If they wouldn't agree, he said he'd take them down to the Ohio River himself.) The deacons took them all, and after the ceremony, people stood up and clapped, came up to meet the students, and told Dwain, "That was so great!"

- The Asbury College revival was on everyone's mind. It began with a one-hour chapel service on February 3, 1970, and ran for one hundred eighty-five hours. People were also aware of the Kent State shootings that occurred May 4, 1970. And the Jesus Movement was well underway, with as many as five hundred baptized in Pirate's Cove by Chuck Smith's Calvary Chapel, Costa Mesa, California. All this contributed to the spiritual ferment at Marshall.

- For witnessing on campus, he used certain key verses, such as those in the Campus Crusade for Christ's tract, *The Four Spiritual Laws*.

- In those days, Navigators, BSU, and Campus Crusade were working in close cooperation. All told, he estimates that there were over a thousand conversions on campus, two hundred of them through the BSU. And of the BSU group, four men became pastors.

- BSU stayed busy, eagerly inviting students to a Tuesday night Bible study, Friday worship, and various noon meetings, where they charged twenty-five cents for a sandwich and coke.

- Gregory recalls wearing a coat and tie to his first BSU meeting at Marshall, but seeing hippies (and casually dressed students there), he never wore a tie to the meeting again.

- For outings, they'd been going to a retreat center in Ohio, but in the summer of 1971, they chose to head up the East Coast, from Maryland to New York, where they had their retreat at a United Nations church.

- In his seminary days at SWBTS, he was discipled by Fred Swank, who shepherded many into the pastorate, including SBC Guidestone president O.S. "Butch" Hawkins, who was in Dwain's seminary class.

- In student ministry, he was a Max Barnett disciple. Max was the BSU director at the University of Oklahoma, where his program was so rigorous that it was imitated throughout the Southern Baptist Convention, with a notable offshoot at Kansas State University. Subsequently, the Baptist Sunday School Board commissioned Max to write a supplement to the denomination's student ministry handbook.

Again, Gregory was active in Westmoreland Baptist Church (American Baptist), where he sang while Jim Fugate (college Sunday School teacher and Dwayne's successor as BSU director at Marshall) accompanied him on the piano. Fugate remembers an old Southern Baptist preacher who'd come to the church for a series of revival services, one who said that "every church needs a kindling group." A young member, Steve Howerton, suggested that Westmoreland should start one, and Fugate volunteered to host such a gathering in his home, with as many as fifty students in attendance.[80] Howerton, who entered Marshall in 1971, recalls baptisms in the Memorial Fountain and a number of BSU students who went on to become pastors.[81] Fugate speaks of his "treasured time" as BSU director, remembering particularly his prayer ministry with students, attending to as many as twenty-five confidential requests at a time.

Arthur Blessitt

The February 26, 1971, *Parthenon* announced a visit by peripatetic evangelist Arthur Blessitt. The twenty-nine year old preacher was known for having established a ministry on Los Angeles's Sunset Strip, one called His Place, "where kids could come in off the street, eat sandwiches and drink coffee, and hear about Christ." The whole thing began in a discotheque, which provided him room for a midnight service, but Blessitt was soon able to acquire a building for his work and to also establish a House of Disciples, also in Los Angeles, where new Christians could go to get their bearings in preparation for witness in the world.

In 1968, Blessitt began a program of city-by-city evangelism, traveling from one to another carrying a ten-foot, eighty-pound cross. (By 2020, he had walked with this cross over forty-three thousand miles, visiting and witnessing in three hundred twenty-four "countries, island groups and territories." And, yes, he made it into the Guinness book.) Along the way, in early 1971, he spoke in the CCC on Sunday morning and made himself available for follow-up conversations at 1670 Sixth Avenue. (Regrettably, Blessitt's ministry was marred by an affair and divorce in 1990, but he remarried that same year and has continued his journeys for the three decades since then.)

Bob Harrington

The fall of 1971 saw more coverage of evangelical happenings in the *Parthenon*. For instance, in the September 2 issue, Sherry Young and Julia Winnings wrote of an impending, local evangelistic crusade led by the "Chaplain of the French Quarter's Bourbon Street," Bob Harrington, at the behest of the Christian Businessmen's Association.

Running the first week of September, with several sessions in the Marshall University field house, the meeting featured a testimony by athletic director Joe McMullen on the night the football team members were special guests. (Earlier in the week, Harrington had donned a Marshall football helmet when he spoke to the football team in a special session.) The series started on Saturday night at Huntington East High School "with a rally attended by over 1,000 students," and on Sunday, he had services at Highlawn Baptist Church and Johnson Memorial Methodist.

Dr. Stephen Beull, director of the University's educational radio and TV program was an enthusiastic supporter. He called the event "an experience the students should not deny themselves," noting that "we have many MU students who are either serving as counselors or as choir members in the 300-member choir." He continued, "The response from the young people has been fantastic. Not only are students helping in the crusade, but many are making public decisions for Jesus . . . some accepting for the first time and others rededicating their lives to Him." Which was well in line with Harrington's key message: "Get saved. Live like it and win others to Jesus Christ."

The article identified three campus groups—Baptist Student Union, Navigators, and Campus Crusade for Christ—as part of the Jesus Movement, and said that Harrington was for "any movement that edifies and lifts up the Lord." But he was a little leery of the name, in that it suggested that a breakthrough had occurred: "Jesus began the movement when he left heaven 2,000 years ago and came to earth. That's the real Jesus Movement . . . We just have new ways of describing ways that God wants us to live."

Then, playing off a current Broadway rock-opera, Harrington said of young people, "Finally, they've gotten around to identifying with the right Superstar. His name is Jesus Christ . . . The people who wrote it, wrote it for money purposes. It doesn't stick to scripture or lift up the Lord like it should." He added that it "needs prayer," but, at least, "it's a good way to get excited about Jesus."

He also talked about a project with David Wilkerson, founder of Times Square Church and Teen Challenge—a "T (Transformatory) House," an "in-between house for the new convert to his new way of life."

(In 1978, Harrington, like Blessitt, had a moral failure, and was out of fellowship with the Lord and his church for several years. But his repentance and restoration are testimony to the grace of God, the dramatic story recounted in an interview with *SBC LIFE*, "Chastened Chaplain: A Forthright Account of Failure and Renewal.")[82]

Ross Rhoads

That same month, September 19–26, evangelist Ross Rhoads returned to the area, leading a crusade with services at Beverly Hills United Methodist Church and Twentieth Street Baptist Church, with other appearances in the Memorial Student Center multi-purpose room and some local high school assemblies. (This was the same Ross Rhoads who'd impacted Alan Wild's life the previous year.) Rhoads's musical accompanist, Ted Cornell, served with the Associated Crusade program the Billy Graham Association.

Rhoads had a degree in philosophy from Wheaton and one in divinity from Fuller. He'd "been involved in youth oriented preaching and counseling in seven countries, military installations, refugee camps, as well as churches and schools." From his base in Valley Forge, Pennsylvania, he traveled as minister-at-large and president of Church Centered Evangelism. The organization's board of reference included such evangelical luminaries as Harold Ockenga (president of Gordon-Conwell), V. Raymond Edman (president of Wheaton College), and Charles E. Fuller (namesake of Fuller Seminary).

Rhoads went on to pastor Calvary Church in Charlotte, North Carolina for two decades, and died May 24, 2017. At Rhoads's 1973 installation as pastor in Charlotte, Billy Graham served as the keynote speaker. In 1992, Rhoads resigned the pastorate to co-found, with Norm Geisler, Southern Evangelical Seminary. He became the first president and Geisler the first dean. "Pastor Rhoads's" burden for evangelism and Professor Geisler's concern to defend the historic Christian faith combined in "the two-fold vision of the seminary to evangelize the world and to defend the historic Christian faith." In October 2008, the Seminary dedicated the Ross Rhoads Center for Evangelism, a fitting tribute since he had traveled the world for more than twenty-five years and had conducted over two hundred crusades. Along the way, he also served as chaplain for the Billy Graham Evangelistic Association, as vice chairman for Samaritan's Purse, and as co-author with Franklin Graham of the devotional book, *All for Jesus*.

Carl F. H. Henry

The September 23, 1971 issue of *The Parthenon* announced two CCC talks by Carl Ferdinand Howard Henry, one at 11:00 ("The Future of Religion") and one at 8:00 ("Christianity and the Youth Counter-Culture"). The following day, Friday, Henry addressed a noon luncheon for faculty at the CCC, the topic, "Christian Witness on Campus." And that evening, he spoke to a public convocation on "Keeping the Barbarians at Bay." (It's likely that there was a fair amount of overlap with Duncan Williams's notion of who the barbarians might be.)

The bio sketch run in the campus paper suggested a seriously non-Woodstockian frame of mind:

> Carl Henry, author of 18 books and editor-at-large of "Christianity Today", began writing on "The Smithtown Star" and "Port Jefferson Times-Echo." He was suburban correspondent for "The New York Times," "New York Herald-Tribune," and "Chicago Tribune."

He was ordained to the Baptist ministry in 1941 at the American Baptist Convention. His latest books include "The God Who Shows Himself," "Evangelicals at the Brink of Crisis," and "Faith at the Frontiers." Syracuse University Library established a Carl F. H. Henry manuscript collection in 1968. Henry headed the Mid-Century Rose Bowl Rally in Pasadena, 1952, and served several years as the chairman of the annual Rose Bowl Easter Sunrise Service. He was chairman of the World Congress on Evangelism, Berlin, Germany, 1966, and was the key speaker at Eastern European Congress on Evangelism, Novi Sad, Yugoslavia, 1969. Henry received Freedoms Foundation award medal in 1954 for a magazine article, "Christianity and the American Heritage," in 1966 for an editorial, "A World Short of Breath," and in 1968 for an editorial on the Vietnam war. Henry has lectured in colleges, seminaries, Bible conferences, and churches in the U.S. and Canada. He has also done radio and television ministries such as "God and Man in the Twentieth Century," a series of 13 television panel discussions shown in the U.S.

Among the things not mentioned (because they had not yet appeared) were his magisterial, six-volume work, *God, Revelation, and Authority* (published from 1976 through 1983) and his endorsements of the *Chicago Statement on Biblical Inerrancy* (1978) and the *Chicago Statement on Biblical Hermeneutics* (1982).

It bears saying that, in terms of biblical and systematic theology, Carl Henry was the antithesis of Louis Jennings, who led religious instruction on the Marshall faculty for over three decades (1948–1979). Though Henry's visit spanned only two days, perhaps it had some impact, perhaps a touch of encouragement for those who believed one could be an accomplished scholar, a biblical inerrantist, a responsible citizen, and a evangelistic "fisher of men" at the same time.

So the evangelical/evangelistic/revivalistic presence was strong in Huntington in those days, a point underscored by a simple announcement in the September 23, 1971 *Parthenon*, one inviting students to an organizational meeting of "Broadcasting for Jesus."

FCA's Loren Young (and AD Joseph McMullen)

In the fall, Loren Young, national director of special programs for the Fellowship of Christian Athletes visited town, an event announced by

Marshall's athletic director, Joseph McMullen, who was serving on FCA's national board of directors. In town to preach for a revival meeting at Johnson Memorial Church, Young was also slated for introduction at a Marshall football game. As McMullen explained in his invitation, Young's sponsor, the FCA, "is not an assembly of saints—just ordinary sinners. We get together for inspiration and perspiration and hope to show young men they can be competitive athletes and witnessing Christians."

Young had been a track star at Huntington high school and then the captain of the track team at Duke, where he went on to coach before receiving a BD from Emory and a DD from West Virginia Wesleyan. In August, the month before coming to Marshall, Young spoke at an FCA gathering of nearly five hundred in Estes Park, Colorado, a meeting covered by Peter Vecsey for the *New York Times*.[83]

Begun in 1947, FCA had, by 1971, grown to fifty-thousand members, many of them famous, e.g., Bill Bradley of the Knicks, Tom Landry of the Cowboys, and Brooks Robinson of the Orioles. Vecsey quoted Young to say, "Let's face it, many of you are heroes," if not on a national stage, at least in their home towns, so they would be carefully scrutinized for their behavior both on and off the field, and also have prominent platforms for witness.

In an October 14 *Parthenon* article, based on an interview, Chuck Landon, homed in on two issues—Young's concern over "dehumanization" of the athlete, by which he or she becomes only a number or a uniform color, and Young's impatience with short-hair codes. Regarding the latter, he said, "It's become so absurd in so many of the evaluations . . . of human character that it's almost like we've made the barber the priest, because his clippers can change the world. Cut a man's hair and he's a different person? . . . [I]t's not so."

Campus Ministry

Campus ministry, which centered on the Campus Christian Center, was typically less evangelistic than the Harrington and Rhoads programs. They were more focused on discussion, ecumenism, and social action. And it's not clear to what extent this was an outworking of their denominational priorities or a response to the late-sixties social tumult in the nation and on campus, or both. And the question stands: Were they mirroring and coping with the culture, or helping to shape it in ways not endearing to the churches from which the students came.

According to the May 11 *Parthenon*, "Turnout was low, but emotions were high" at a commemorative gathering on the first anniversary of the May 7, Kent State shootings. Rev. Bill Miller, the United Methodist campus minister stirred the crowd, "I have in mind hundreds of thousands of reasons why we should be here today. Four of them are the four lives at Kent State." He added that they should also consider the "hundreds of thousands" who have "died morally" in support of the Vietnam War.

George Sublette and Presbyterian Campus Minister, Hardin "Corky" King, were also involved in a CCC spring event, dedicated to the work of the controversial Catholic priest Teilhard de Chardin (specifically his book *The Phenomenon of Man*), of whom Pope John XXIII's Vatican said it is "obvious that in philosophical and theological matters, the said works are replete with ambiguities or rather with serious errors which offend Catholic doctrine." Chardin, with a background in paleontology and geology, used evolution as the model for his theology and helped inspire the New Age movement. Nevertheless, "Corky" King called him "an outstanding scientist and priest" who was "trying to make sense of the whole cosmic process." For this respectful series of lectures, King enlisted Sublette, Louis Jennings (chairman of the Bible and religion department), Howard Slaatte (chairman of the philosophy department), and Robert Staley (graduate student in philosophy).

Catholic House

Perhaps the tone of the CCC (which could sponsor a series devoted to a priest who was denied teaching positions at Catholic universities and whose works were shunned by Catholic bookstores) helped nudge Marshall University Catholics to establish their own separate center in a converted eight-room house across Fifth Street and a bit west of the CCC. In the spring of 1971, a parish council made up of thirty Catholic students and faculty member at Marshall inaugurated the Marshall Catholic House.

In doing so, they took pains to say they weren't breaking ties with or withdrawing support from the CCC. Indeed, they were pleased to say that sophomore Penny Derenge would serve dually as president of the MCH and the first student member of the CCC.

This was a sensitive matter, a point reflected in the April 15, 1971, *Parthenon*, when freshman Betsy Greenwell responded to a critical letter penned by John G. F. Littler, assistant professor chemistry:

I was shocked by his rather arrogant statement which consigns those who believe in the existence of God to a level of timidity and limited perception. I was also surprised that an Atheist would be concerned with the location of Catholic devotions.

The Catholic church drew his criticism for supposedly withdrawing from the Campus Christian Center and neglecting its ecumenical duty. True, the Catholic Community has purchased a house; however, it will continue to use and financially support the Campus Christian Center. Also, as a former Catholic, I am sure Dr. Littler is aware that ecumenism has its natural limits.

As a Catholic, I feel I have the right and the responsibility to voice my position. There appears in his writing a somewhat harsh intolerance toward those whose belief in a deity he calls into question. As a man of scientific method, I would like to have him logically derive his conclusion of the non-existence of God, so that all of us can share his insight from soundly reasoned ground.

The new Catholic chapel was dedicated to those who died in the plane crash. With white walls and green carpeting, it featured a range of items connected with the tragedy, including a chalice donated by the parents of Kevin Gilmore and its tray given by Kevin's girlfriend Kathy Dial; an ornately carved crucifix, from Germany's Black Forest, a gift of Mrs. Gene Morehouse; a "Twelfth Man" sticker on the door, referring to God, according to chaplain Scott.

Perhaps picking up the evangelical revival, Father Scott initiated a program to unite "Jesus Freaks" and "Jesus Squares," both groups "sincerely concerned with the Jesus movement" (*Parthenon,* June 24). It had a defensive tone to it, for he expressed the fear that "an overnight success would not be lasting and solid." On his model, the meetings would be open to all, relaxed, and informal, so as to encourage discussion. He added, "I would be there to serve as a guide. I do not wish to control these meetings. I would only be there to keep 'self-appointed Messiahs' from taking over."

Transcendental Meditation and Yoga

Christianity wasn't the only religious interest on campus. The April 2, 1971, *Parthenon* reports on a lecture series on Transcendental Meditation, hosted by local coordinator, sophomore English major Joel Wallis. Claiming sixty thousand meditators on six hundred campuses, the Student International Meditation Society embraced and amalgamated the teachings of "Lord

Krishna," "Lord Buddha," and "Lord Jesus Christ," with commentary and application by Maharishi Mahesh Yogi. At Marshall, around twenty attended the lecture, and eleven signed up to continue the course, at a cost of $35.

The next month, Swami (i.e., a Hindu male religious teacher) Hyder Shah, an India-born sociology professor at the University of Kentucky, came to campus to train people in the way to tranquility without sedatives. Although Hindu, his presentation was delivered in the CCC, with the focus on yoga, "the practice of complete concentration upon something to establish identity of consciousness." He explained to the group of about twenty students and one faculty member that "the first rule in achieving true bliss of the physical, mental and spiritual, is to regard the human body as a 'temple to God.'"

He then led the group through a series of breathing and stretching exercises, which led one student to observe, "I feel strangely relaxed and limber, but at the same time, very revived." Interest was sufficient for Shah to agree to return weekly, and, for $35 a student, he led them through a ten-week course, employing as many as three hundred different yoga positions.

The "Edgy" Annuals

Issues of the *Chief Justice* in the 1960s would flirt with impropriety (e.g., coverage of the Tau Kappa Epsilon "Playboy" house party, with waitresses sporting rabbit ears), but the 1970 and 1971 issues took matters to a different level, parading liberation from decorum (or parading conformity to "liberation" fashion) in a variety of ways, photos taking the lead—a jock strap taped to a brick wall, with "Give Xavier a 'Young Thundering Hernia' "; a two-page spread with a wine bottle, three bar scenes, and a student doing his business at a urinal; four students at a ball game wearing "MAC [Mid-America Conference] SUCKS" tee-shirts; a student smoking weed on a "Spring Break" page; the image of a woman student taking a shower, seen through a textured, translucent door; a photo-negative image of a nude male student toweling off in the locker room; a rear photo of a nude coed in the woods.

Apparently the laissez-faire take on drugs reflected in the yearbook was, indeed, normative in a wide swath of the student body. The 1971 yearbook reports, with a two-page photo spread, on the evening of October 8, 1970:

> A feeling of tenseness connected with Molotov cocktails, the
> chants of the participants, breaking of windows, and the burning

of trailers, plus the menacing troopers—gas masks—rifles—soon brought a non-bloody confrontation sparing us a Kent State but giving us a mayor's overaction. A balmy evening of a few dozen students' violence, and 2000 onlookers' pastime, an evening in the aftermath of drug raids, an evening of rage and bitterness and alleged police excesses . . .

(In a May 17, 1971 article, "MU '70–71 in retrospect," *Parthenon* feature writer, Mike Torlone, supplied the figures—25 persons were "arrested in an outbreak of violence, reportedly triggered by the arrest of 10 persons, including three Marshall students the previous night on drug charges.")

"A Great Awakening on Campus"

In the September 22, 1971 issue of *The Parthenon*, we read a letter from Huntington junior Bob Jones, one bearing the heading, "Student looks at religion":

There is a growing awareness, not only on this campus, but all across this nation of the claims of Jesus Christ. People everywhere seem to be taking a closer look at the greatest revolutionary of all time, the one who claimed to be God in the flesh.

What about that? How could anyone be God in the flesh and walk the earth and tell us the only way to heaven was through Him? Man, was He crazy or was He who He said He was, the son of God?

What makes people afraid to talk about Jesus? Say that name, Jesus. There's something special about that name because it represents a sacrifice so beautiful and fantastic it's almost beyond comprehension. Jesus Christ died for each and every one of us so that we may have eternal life. Man is separated from God by his sinful nature, yet he is continually trying to reach that right relationship with his Creator.

Deep inside every person is a need and want for that relationship, a personal relationship between man and God. Man reaches but he is separated from God by the barrier of sin. God knew man could never reach him because of his sin so He sent His son Jesus Christ, to wipe away the sin. Yes, God loved you and me so much that He let his son die a horrible death for us, and do we really deserve it?

Jesus died, but death could not hold him. He arose into life and conquered death. He lives so we may live also.

Many people are so worried they will have to give up something when they accept Christ into their lives that they keep putting it off. It's not a matter of giving anything up. It's just having the faith to ask Jesus into your life and then letting Him have control.

He is a living God and He can live in your life, directing it and giving you true peace and happiness. **There has been a great awakening on this campus. Can you feel it?**

Jesus Christ is pulling at your heart. There are some who laugh now, but as you laugh and as you start to lay the paper aside ask yourself if Jesus was crazy or was He truly who he said He was. Because if He is the son of God, He offers you the most wonderful plan of life imaginable.

You say I'm a crazy preaching fanatic? People get pretty fanatical about beer on campus, student elections, the Vietnam War and the MAC, but I'm hung up on something that is the same yesterday, today, and forever. If I'm fanatical, it's a lasting cause, an everlasting cause I'm proud to be fanatical about. I know all things will pass away, but the love of God for me and you is forever and He will never leave me because I have Him in my heart.

10

The Years Since

THIS BOOK APPEARS IN 2020, fifty years after the crash, and one despairs of doing those intervening decades justice. Still, the story continues, just as surely as the sovereign and providential hand of God (and the machinations of The Old Deluder) continue to manifest themselves in this place.

Kenovans

The story of this book was essentially, at first impression, one of a campus revival sparked by soul-searching in the wake of a tragedy, but it soon became clear that gratifying spiritual developments were underway in the preceding years, and, as noted below, in the succeeding years. So 1971 was not an isolated phenomenon, but one sitting center of mass in a cluster of phenomena that blessed the campus and community.

Syd Wheeler, the last religion major on campus before the department was phased out, has vivid memories of those years. As he recalls, "things were being prepared" before the crash, notably at First Baptist Church, Kenova, where the youth music program was stout in that era. Michael W. Smith, who studied at Marshall before leaving for a remarkable career in the music industry, was in that choir. With fifty to sixty voices and a budget larger than that of the city, they traveled far and wide, including a concert at an Air Force base in Florida in 1972. They worked out of a Cliff Barrows songbook, accompanied by drums and guitars, which are now commonplace, but not so much back then. They even sang on the Marshall campus in connection with Ross Rhoads's preaching. And yes, there was a charismatic element to their zeal as many "sought tongues and healing."

Wheeler remembers his own zeal, manifested in his wearing a six-inch long metal cross, his purchase of the biggest Scofield Bible he could find, and his indifference to being called a "Jesus Freak." It was a time of house-based Bible studies, as groups would gather frequently at a "spiritual haven" or "refreshing station." Focus ranged from the Psalms to Hal Lindsey's *The Late, Great Planet Earth* (sparking pre-mill/post-mill/a-mill discussions), all undergirded with prayer and fueled by a range of Bible translations. "Wanting to be there all the time," one group of up to twenty kids met several nights a week, eventually wearing out the host.[84]

The Liberated *Chief Justice*

The university yearbook was called *Mirabilia* until 1933, and then, after a seven year break, it reemerged as *The Chief Justice*. Throughout the 1970s, it was clear that the school and the editors had drunk deeply from the sixties, reflecting the spirit of "Captain America" (Peter Fonda) in *Easy Rider* as well as the protagonists of such turn-of-the-decade offerings as *Zabriskie Point*, *Billy Jack*, and *The Strawberry Statement*.

Of course, there was plenty of the classic yearbook fare, but the editorial tone was unmistakably "counter-culture," with a counter-traditional-Christianity flavor. Here's a sampling:

- fascination with streaking, yielding full, rear-end shots and a spicy cartoon, with four coeds exclaiming as a nude guy ran by, "I guess we know who's the big man on campus now!" (1974); scenes of midnight streaking, with certain parts covered (1975) and then not covered, with full frontal male nudity (1976)

- a marijuana plant growing under a desk lamp and a student's "snorting black hash" in a dorm room (1976)

- Kit Roberts, a freshman, bemoaning the fact that they're told to grow up and act like adults, but they're not treated like adults, e.g., permitted alcohol and after-hours guests of the opposite sex in the dorms; but with a word of appreciation for compensatory comfort, in that they got to go bar hopping and "ripping off the Pepsi machine" for some excitement (1976)

- a survey of the "drinking, dancing" aspects of student "night life" and the report that Huck Finn's lost its liquor license "as a result of complaints against 'rowdy students'" (1977); a GDI ("God Damned Independent," i.e., non-Greek) keg party chased out of a city park, where beer had been banned by city ordinance (1978); and, that same year, an article dealing with Marshall's deserved reputation as a "party school"

- a blank page, with only the words "this page has been—blurp-zip-expletive deleted—partially erased in honor of the current administration" (1974)

- a two-page, six-photo spread on Hiram Hill and Sandy Bryant, who were co-habiting without benefit of marriage (illegal in West Virginia at the time), the "scandal" multiplied by the fact that he was black and she white; Sandy's observations that "The piece of paper wouldn't make any difference anyway"; the yearbook's note that they learned it "was economically useful since their social security and VA checks would be less if they were married"; and, Sandy's glad report, "We really get to know each other this way."

- a student in an off-campus apartment shown beaming as he reads an issue of *Playboy* (1978).

CCC's Center for Simulation Studies

Coordinated by William D. Miller, the Center for Simulation Studies was housed in and sponsored by the Campus Christian Center. It offered "a wide variety of structured human relations experiences and simulation games, personal growth, group development, and a better understanding of our socio-cultural environment." These simulation games made "learning fun" by offering "a combination of role play, chance and control" providing "a quick overview of actual life situations," making way for "experimentation where the player can make 'low-cost' mistakes instead of 'high-cost' real life mistakes." The games typically engaged around ten players and ran an hour and a half, but one (*West Virginia*) could handle a hundred players and extend for several days.

- *Blacks and Whites*: "You may end up on welfare, bankrupt, or in white suburbia. The challenge of the black minority is to keep the land-hungry majority from winning quickly and to shake up the status quo."

- *Cities*: "Assuming the roles of business, government, slum dwellers and agitators, players participate in power struggles as they seek the difficult but essential cooperation that will avoid the disintegration of their city."

- *Ecology Games*: namely "The Pollution Game," "Man and His World," and "Build an Incinerator"

- *Edge City College*: "The players are given administrative, faculty, and student roles and then subjected to the pressures and frustrations found in a typical university."

- *Ghetto*: "Each player is given a different ghetto role and attempts to improve his role by investing time-chips within the constraints of the ghetto economic and educational systems."

- *Human Relations-Group Development*: including the games, "Broken Squares," "Instant Insanity," "Pick a Color," "Build a Tower," and "Win as Much as You Can"—games designed to "help a group of people learn to work together"

- *New Town*: ". . . pits Greed against Environmentalists."

- *Starpower*: "A 3-tiered society with unequal distribution of wealth and power is simulated through a trading process."

- *The Value Game*: "This game attempts to understand the lack of ethical consensus among any randomly selected group and to see the resultant inadequacy of a moral-ethical system which affirms moral absolutes."

- *West Virginia*: "Taking the roles of various power and powerless groups in West Virginia," it "demonstrates well the complexity of the social change process in Appalachia."

- *Youth Culture Game*: "The purpose of this game is to simulate the world of youth, to participate in and evaluate new life styles, and to create an experience in which players are actively involved in bridging the generation gap."

At base, these reflected the mindset of "critical theory," reading society through the lens of power struggles, siding with the ubiquitous oppressed against the oppressors. This program continued the "social approach" of George Sublette, and with an obvious social agenda not congenial to the thinking of many Christians. Among the dissenters would be the evangelical environmentalists in the Cornwall Alliance and the Catholic, free-market capitalists of the Acton Institute.

Black Students

On into the sixties, the term "Negro" was still current, as evidenced through its use by such edgy Impact speakers as Malcolm Boyd and Dick Gregory, and, indeed, by Martin Luther King. Today, that word is rarely used, and the expressions "African-American" and "Person of Color" are common. But in the 1970s, "Black" was preferred by far, occurring frequently in *The Parthenon*, as in the black-awareness issue (April 30, 1971), with Angela Dodson (quoted below) as special editor. Though Jim Crow had run afoul of the law in the 1960s, there was still much dissatisfaction among blacks on the Marshall campus, as is obvious from these representative comments in that issue (with frequent uses of the "N word" avoided):

- From "Social life—What is that? Ask blacks on campus": Toni Davis observed, "Blacks are neither seen nor heard; he's just not here as far as the white man is concerned, that is unless he bothers whitey."

- From "Black attitude negative but certain justified": Mel Glatt, a white student, reports, "Apparently, the majority of black students on this campus feel . . . that Marshall lags far behind other institutions of higher learning in resolving its racial conflicts rather [sic] it be of a social or education [sic] nature."

- From "A black looks at clichés": Gaylord Stewart lists ten, including "4. Some of my best friends are colored" (A: "So what?"); "5. What do they want? (A: "If you knew, you might get angry—or scared."); "7. Why do they drive Cadillacs?" (A: "They say in Harlem the going thing is an air-conditioned Volkswagen (Thank God)."

- "Free Angela": Angela Dodson argued that Marxist philosopher Angela Davis had been fired and framed because "some Californians reasoned (a mockery of the word) that since all Communists are dangerous and all blacks are dangerous, then [she was] an evil risk and an unfit influence on growing minds. This being too much for white capitalist Americans to stomach."

- "Black Man" and "The Degree": The same Angela Dodson waxed poetic with such lines as "Black man, Dark man, King of joy, Prince of Sorrow, Man with one foot in Hell, Man whose spirit is almost crushed ..." and "Bachelor of Blackness, School of soul, Ghetto University, Major in hardship, Minor in deprivation, With a concentration in basic starvation, Also received an honorary license to be lynched."

- "To be understood is to be beautiful": In an article by Angela Dodson, sophomore Lee Ernest McClinton is quoted to say, "I see few advances at Marshall, constructively speaking. I see no recruitment of black faculty or students, no substantial curriculum, only a few token courses, and no concerted effort made to release students of their ignorance [about black awareness]. They [educators] don't see black culture as a part of American society. They try sometimes, but they don't do the right thing."

The University had instituted a Student Relations Center and a Black Awareness Week including, for instance (in 1972), a gospel sing on Sunday, lawyer-activist speaker Florynce Kennedy on Monday, the movie *Cotton Comes to Harlem* on Tuesday, the West Virginian State ROTC glee club on Thursday, a talent show on Friday, the Afro Ball on Saturday, and various art exhibits on Sunday, Tuesday, and Wednesday. The B.U.S. (Black United Students) chapter fielded forty-eight students in the 1970 yearbook picture, the same issue showing black students with outthrust or upraised fists. Yearbooks also featured group photos of black fraternities (Omega Psi Phi and Kappa Alpha Psi) and sororities (Delta Sigma Theta and Alpha Kappa Alpha). Despite Lee McClinton's complaint that there were "only a few token courses" on the topic, *The Parthenon* reports that by April of 1971, there were thirteen courses involving seven departments in the program, the first appearing in 1968–1969 (Negro Culture in America). Thirty-five students enrolled in that initial course, and the campus FREE group (Freedom and Racial Equality for Everyone) encouraged the formation of a black studies program, a request well-received by the academic vice president.

Although the civil rights movement of the 1960s was eager to saturate their work with scripture (e.g., as by Fred Shuttlesworth, Ralph Abernathy, and MLK), this didn't seem to be the strong suit of movement leaders on campus, at least as portrayed in university publications. While the 1971 awareness week was kicked off with gospel singing, the week's featured speaker was an atheist who, as a longtime champion of grievance-intersectionality, was openly contemptuous of the church. As Florynce Kennedy put it (cleverly if not fairly), "It's interesting to speculate how it developed that in two of the most anti-feminist institutions, the church and the law court, the men are wearing the dresses."

Bob Bondurant Remembers

Bob Bondurant served as both Presbyterian campus minister and, for a time, team chaplain (with a national championship rign to show for it). Over his twenty-three years of campus ministry, he saw thirty-four ministers emerge from his group, including Gusti Newquist, who later attended Harvard Divinity School. At her eponymous website, we read that she "is a poet, a preacher, a teacher, and a healer," who "offers caring, contemplative presence for people of all spiritual traditions (or none) reflecting on life's deep questions." Then, as a "ritualist," she "works with clients to develop group or individual ceremonies to guide them through major life transitions: weddings, funerals, coming of age ceremonies, divorce rituals, women's group activities, and more."

Gusti credits Bob with turning her toward campus ministry:

> I intended to remain what is now termed "spiritual but not religious" until pure peer pressure led me to the Presbyterian Campus Ministry at Marshall University in Huntington, West Virginia. First, I was drawn into the social ministries of the group: visiting nursing homes and providing activities for teenagers who had been removed from their schools by the court system. Then, I was drawn into the possibility of "a thinking faith" that invited more and more questions in exchange for "pat answers." Finally, I was drawn into deep love and caring offered by the campus minister to students across a very dramatic theological spectrum, love and caring that I ultimately understand came directly from an experience of the living God.[85]

Bondurant remembers George Chaump, who coached Marshall (1986–1989), where he enjoyed back-to-back ten-win seasons. Though a Presbyterian like Bondurant, he didn't want a team chaplain, for he was fearful of divisiveness.[86] Chaump was succeeded by Jim Donnan, who coached Marshall for six years beginning in 1990, and who led the team to an NCAA 1-AA championship in 1992. Donnan was "crusty . . . crude, rough," with "nothing to do with faith." He prompted fights on Friday to tune the players up for Saturday. Still, Bondurant saw another side, when Donnan cried as an Army player died on the field and when he got news of a kid involved in a car wreck.

Bob Pruett (1996–2004) brought the team to an extraordinary record of success, including a .803 winning record, two undefeated seasons, and a NCAA 1-AA championship in 1996. Along the way, he coached such Marshall luminaries as Randy Moss, Chad Pennington, and Brian Leftwich. Bondurant clicked with Pruett, who supported Fellowship of Christian Athletes and would accompany the thirty to forty players who came to the Campus Christian Center for a service after a game-day meal, whether breakfast or lunch. (He never required attendance.) African-American players would sing, and the gathering was open to all (including coaches and parents), with around ninety in attendance. On the road, they would gather in a large hotel room, and he had different players lead in prayer. (In Donnan's era, they also had services, with fifteen to twenty players in attendance.)

Bondurant's football "parish" was fraught with challenges. During his tenure, three players saw their parents shot to death in their houses. There was poverty and a sense of fatalism in their background. One player was living a loose life and confided in Bondurant that it would kill his preacher father if he knew what he was up to. Bob talked with him about the loss of his mother and how it had impacted him. And Randy Moss was a challenge himself. He had some rough edges when he came to Marshall, but a turning point came when he befriended a religious guy with a brain tumor, and he visited him every day. Occasionally you would see Randy at chapel, but that wasn't a big interest of his. Later on, at the 2000 reunion, he approached Bob with "It would be nice if you led us in prayer." (Incidentally, the Winter 2000 issue of *Marshall* magazine mentioned that Moss had, several years earlier, visited an orphanage/clinic in Mexico with members of Charleston's Fellowship of Christian Athletes.)

Another preacher's son, Doug Chapman, started drinking and missing chapel, and his father called, "Please help." There was gradual improvement, and he turned to Bob for help on the sidelines: "Pray for me during the game when I come off the field between series." So Bob got on his knees on a wet day. There was no gain on the next play, and Chapman said, "You've got to have a better prayer than that." Then, after a three-yard gain, they got on their knees again. And this time, he responded with a seventy-five-yard run and a touchdown, a hundred-yard-plus day. Later, at the Motor City Bowl, Bondurant was going to ask Chad Pennington to speak, but he turned to Doug for a word about his growth. For the first time, he offered a prayer, a sweet one including a plea, "Help us love and serve you." Doug ended up going eighty yards for the winning touchdown, winning the MVP award.

Bondurant also remembers a player who was on the brink of suicide, having had a bad day with his girlfriend. He had a shotgun in his truck, and Bob got in with him for a ride around. They talked about the nature of chronic depression, and he persuaded him to check in with the team doctor. Prozac helped him get back on track.

There was always the call to minister to those with physical injuries, at least one a day, some of them career ending., e.g., a torn ACL. It was very stressful. In that connection, Bob found the expectations of "Fundamentalists" to be a challenge, in that they were primed to "expect a miracle and the chaplain to perform it."

Coach Mark Snyder (2005–2009), a 1988 Marshall graduate, was a standout player in his days with the Thundering Herd. Bondurant remembers him as young, handsome, and well-spoken. "A gung-ho Baptist," he chose to replace Bondurant with his high school chaplain, and he shifted services to the facilities building, with only the team in attendance, meeting at night after movies.

In 1995, on the twenty-fifth anniversary observance of the crash, Bonderant delivered a "Prayer of the People." At that same service Elizabeth Ward, Keith Morehouse and Nate Ruffin offered reflections. (Both Ward and Morehouse lost their fathers in the crash, and an injured Ruffin didn't make the trip.) The Black United Students Mass Choir sang a number, a wreath was laid, "Taps" was sounded, and the Memorial Fountain was turned off for the winter. The late sculptor of the fountain, Harry Bertoia, had said his work was meant for "the living, rather than commemorating Death itself, in the waters of life, rising, renewing, reaching to express upward growth, immortality and eternality."

Bondurant's ministry extended as well to the coaches and their families. He recalls the death of a student in a car crash near Morehead, Kentucky. In the hospital, a young coach hurried to him to ask, "What do I say? What do I do?" And he's been contacted by coaches who've moved on to other positions, with one of them calling him for five years after departure from Marshall.

Chad Pennington's Witness

In Bill Chastain's book, *Purpose and Passion: Bobby Pruett & the Marshall Years*, we don't find explicit reference to God, but his treatment of Chad Pennington underscores Chad's Christian character. For one thing, Chad was humble enough to be "red shirted" his sophomore year, making way for Florida transfer Eric Kresser to assume the role of quarterback. It was tough and a number of key people disagreed with the shift, but, as coach Pruett observed, "Chad is probably the one that made that thing work, because, if he hadn't have done what he did and been acceptable with all that stuff, it wouldn't have worked."[87]

Chad, who went on to lead Marshall football to greater glory and to start for the New York Jets, grants that the year "off" gave him time to bulk and muscle up in his core, while observing that "it wasn't as much strengthening my arm, because I think arm strength is just a God-given talent."[88] Chastain's summary take on Pennington explained why he was known as the "Golden Child": "Not only had Pennington been a standout on the football field, he had also been a star student in the classroom and he constantly was out in the community doing the type of things people dream their football heroes do. In short, Pennington had been the All-American boy."[89]

His successor, Bryan Leftwich, who went on to play for the Jacksonville Jaguars, also sings his praises:

> Chad taught me how to play quarterback . . . [F]or him to do what he did just shows you what type of person Chad was. He was considered by some the best quarterback in college football and at the same time he was still willing and able to try to teach me what he could so I would have an opportunity to be successful. So that was the great thing about Chad. Me and Chad's been friends ever since.[90]

The Summer 1999 issue of *Marshall* magazine notes that "Pennington frequently speaks at schools, charity functions and churches, rarely mentioning that he's a 10,000 yard passer and the most prolific quarterback at a school that has produced seven consecutive all conference passers." Then the Christian, Sports Spectrum ministry picks up on his witness with this video segment, interweaving narrative and testimony:

> In early 2007, after having been the starting quarterback for five seasons, Chad finally found himself benched by coach Eric

Mangini. "That's where I was burned, molded, and tested, and had to go through a lot of different circumstances and truly understand what my purpose was and what am I doing here?" On August 7, 2008, the Jets released Chad Pennington in favor of quarterback Brett Favre. "When I was released, that wasn't the trial. The trial was the year and a half before that. And the release was the oasis, because the year and a half before that was really difficult for me." It was during this time that Chad was forced to reevaluate his life and consider some of things his wife Robin had been telling him for months, that his emphasis on football had gotten out of balance with the rest of his life. "I think I came out of New York a stronger believer, I think I came out New York a more mature adult, and New York helped me put things in perspective as far as my professional life and my family life, and understanding how all that works together . . . Once I was released, really there was a peace about it. There was a sense of calm that the Lord gave me about it, knowing that he's in control, and I know that something good's going to happen. And wherever he has me, there's a reason for it, and I may not understand the reason, and not know the reason, but that's okay.[91]

Et Cetera

But, of course, in the years since the crash, not every Marshall voice has been winsomely Christian. The 1974 issue features photographs of sculpture, one featuring two dogs having sex, and a poem about menstruation, that begins

> When the girl I love
> Falls each month
> Into the absorbent bandages
> Of her gender

And goes downhill from there, not only through the poem, but down through the decade to the spring of 1980, when we come upon a poem appropriately named "blasphemy," by issue editor, Ken Smith. The cover photograph, also by Ken Smith, is entitled *Sex*. It features a woman in a night gown, wearing a monkey mask, sitting on a railroad track in front of a factory.

hi there
lord of all creation
i'd ask, but
i know being an icon must be hard work
thought so
but tell me
for
i've often wondered just how
you get by
like
what do you say when you c[*]m
and does your halo attract moths at night
(unless of course it's yellow)
and
are you a republican
(as everybody says)
and
aside to me
dear lord
what's it like being subject to millions of creators
who say
you look like a painting on a chapel ceiling
(cracked at that)
and
who say
they know your will
and
as a favor to you
enforce it
even when you couldn't care less
so tell me
lordy
don't you get tired of
all this s[**]t
thought so

Professor Simon Perry and Thomas Jefferson's "Big Lie"

In 2016, Simon Perry, professor emeritus of political science, came out with a book built around the Declaration of Independence, one that took issue with it repeatedly. (Perry's forty-eight year tenure at a professor at Marshall was the longest in school history.) In the conclusion, he observed,

The biggest lie is Jefferson's claim that God created the universe and all life within it. While this view is rejected by most scientists today, during the days of Jefferson almost all the people of the world shared this belief, and a small majority still do.[92]

He also found "all created equal" and "self-evident truths" to be bogus, a conviction he likely shared with the twenty-thousand students he taught (at Marshall and two other universities), to whom he dedicated the book. In the bio notes for Marshall University's Simon Perry Center for Constitutional Democracy, we read that he received the Distinguished West Virginian Award and Marshall's Distinguished Faculty Award: "His impact on Marshall and its students has been profound; the Center is designed to continue his legacy." No doubt, true, and often salutary, but not clearly so spiritually.

Spiritually Radioactive Outsiders and Insiders

In recent years, two phenomena demonstrate the range of spiritual and moral takes allowed on campus—or, more properly, one *allowed*, the other *certified*. **First, for the tolerated "extremists"**: In the fall of 2017, two itinerant preachers, Zach Humphrey and John Adkins, came to campus and created quite a stir. (It's reported that they appeared not long after two others whose behavior was so obnoxious that they set the campus, devout Christians included, on edge, even saying such things as "You're a whore and deserved to be raped," but this was not Humphrey's and Adkins's style.) As Humphrey put it, albeit in prickly terms, "I know Jesus Christ, and he said 'go preach to those sinners at Marshall today . . . My purpose here is to convince you that you are hell deserving sinners without Jesus." *The Parthenon* (September 12) shows him wearing a T-shirt with "Trust Jesus" and holding a sign, "Jesus Forgives Sin, Romans 5:8," the flip-side reading, "Jesus Christ, Savior or Judge?"

In the September 12 issue President Jerry Gilbert defended their right to speak in this setting and in this manner (on the land of a state institution and operating under the protection of the First Amendment), recalling a similar phenomenon when he was a freshman at Mississippi State. He reminded the students, "There's always the opportunity to walk by and smile and not say anything and not be offended." Besides, "I feel like if a student came to a college campus and never got to see some extreme person like that on campus, they would have missed out on the college experience."

One student played a saxophone nearby to compete with Humphrey's preaching. Another suggested that he should "preach about God's love and not negative things." In contrast, John McGlone, in a September 29 letter to the editor, pushed back against those who objected to a preacher's harsh talk, noting that Jesus himself spoke of some as "swine"; that rebukes can be the work of love; that Christians should expect to be hated by the world; that the blood of the wicked is on our hands if we don't warn them; and that "Bereans" are willing to test what they're hearing by the standard of God's word.

Second, for the platformed "moderates": Advice columns, featuring the wisdom of *Parthenon* photo editor Alex Runyon ("Ask Alex") and Michael Brown ("xoxo, Michael Brown") would have been scandalous to the university's founders, but their observations enjoyed prominence in the school paper. Here's sampling of Alex's counsel contrary to the clear teaching of the Bible:

- To an anxious virgin—"You should only have sex if you feel safe, comfortable and ready with a consenting adult partner who feels the same way." (September 19, 2017)

- To a student "seeing/sleeping with a 32-year-old, but who wishes a broader day-to-day relationship: "Oh, boy, have I been in your shoes before! This is a common issue, trust me. The days of sock hops and 'going steady' are long gone; I can't remember the last time I heard of someone asking their partner "Will you be my girlfriend?" And there's nothing wrong with that! Putting so much pressure on a relationship-defining conversation can cause undue stress." (September 12, 2017— the same issue covering the furor over campus preachers)

Then there is the "xoxo, Michael Brown" advice column, Brown self-identifying as a "biracial gay male":

- Q—"Have you ever had a one-night stand?"; A—"Please don't judge me, but I'm going to be honest and say yes, I have. I don't regret it; I'm young, living and loving life." (November 15, 2016)

- Q—"Do you think cheating is ever justified?": A—"I mean, sh[*]t happens. If we're talking like on a test, haven't we all done that once before? If you're talking about in a relationship, I can't say it's justified, but it sadly does happen." (November 1, 2016)

- Q—What do you think about religion and science?"; A—"Personally, I'm religious. So I believe in God and the Bible." (January 20, 2016)

- Q—"Are people born homosexual or do they choose to be?"; A—"Why would anyone honestly think someone just wakes up one day and thinks I'm going to be queer? Hands down I believe you're born that way. I know I was." (January 20, 2016)

- Q—"Do you believe in horoscopes?"; A—"Yeah, I actually find the zodiac and that stuff super interesting." (March 10, 2017)

- Q—"What is your opinion about sex on the first date?"; A—I'm not saying to go out on a date with intentions of giving your cookie up, but if the chemistry is there, then go for it." (September 20, 2016)

- Q—"What are your plans after graduating Marshall?"; A—[I] pray I'll be working towards earning my master's degree in marketing at the University of Maryland. After obtaining my MBA, I plan to move into the city and live a Sex and the City lifestyle . . . I just want to live life, travel and experience new things. I'm ready for whatever God has planned for me, I think." (September 13, 2016).

A thought experiment: What if Alex and Michael upset some students by speaking on campus under signs that read, "Don't Let the Bible Pharisees Kill Your Sex Life" and "Homophobes Misread the Bible"? It's likely that President Gilbert would defend their free speech rights. But he doesn't have to. They're already generously exercised in his campus paper.

Another thought experiment: What if someone advocating a chaste, heterosexual—indeed, biblical—sexual ethic as well as Christian orthodoxy which aligned with the historic creeds were granted space for a prominent, regular advice column? Of course, the separation-of-church-and-state crowd would kill that notion, all the while supporting the affronts-to-traditional-Christianity-by-the-state crowd.

Feeding the Narrative

While it would be indecorous to outright dismiss conservative Christianity as toxic, *The Parthenon* was quite happy to take indirect shots at the faith, furthering the narrative that these pious folks are defective—part of the problem rather than part of the solution:

- A half-page report on the fall of an Alabama governor, charged with financial and sexual misbehavior, identified him as a "mild-mannered 74-year-old Republican and one-time Baptist deacon." (April 11, 2017)

- A thirty-column-inch AP report on seventy-year-old Alabama judge Roy Moore (whose run for the U.S. Senate crashed when it was reported that, as a thirty-two-year-old, he showed romantic interest in some teenaged girls), observes that he'd "made his name in Republican politics through his public devotion to hardline Christian conservative positions" and had fought efforts "to remove a 5,200 pound granite Ten Commandments monument from the lobby of the state judicial building . . ." (November 10, 2017)

- In response to "Donald Trump's "lewd" comments, the paper collected anonymous accounts from students and alumni who'd "been assaulted/taken advantage of in vulnerable situations"; in their selection of seven blurbs, the longest concerned a minister in training, who's now a preacher (October 11, 2016).

One wonders whether the paper would have devoted half a page to a scandal involving a Democrat, taking pains to spell out the theological orientation of his or her church of choice.

Memorial Observances at the Fountain

Memorial Services aren't limited to the Fountain. For instance, the parents of Jack Repasy, Bobby Harris, and Mark Andrews (who all played at Cincinnati's Moeller High School), arranged a mass for them each November 14 for years. Also

- Shawna Hattan, cousin of offensive lineman Michael Blake, had "From the ashes we rose" tattooed on her foot. She remembers her first memorial observance, 2007, when someone sang *Amazing Grace* as the fountain was turned off (November 14, 2011).

- The singing of *Amazing Grace* when the fountain is turned off for the winter ("Silencing the Fountain") was commonplace, as was invocation by the football team chaplain/pastor (Bob Bondurant, 2005; Steve Harvey, 2006, 2008) or local minister (Chuck Lawrence, 2007; Samuel Moore, 2009; Allen Meadows, 2010) or campus minister (Dana Sutton, Presbyterian Campus Minister, 2011, 2012, 2013). The same went for the benediction (e.g., Dan Byrd, Revolution Ministries, 2006; Jerry Losh, BCM;)

Such spiritual involvement was too much for the editorial page of *The Parthenon* in its 2014 reflection on that year's memorial gathering, "Don't put religion over unity" (November 17, 2014).

> The 44th annual memorial ceremony to honor the 75 Marshall University football players, staff and members of the community lost in the November 14, 1970, plane crash was a wonderful commemoration of sacrifice and celebration of rebirth.
>
> Overall the ceremony was beautiful. The biggest crowd many of us can remember surrounded the fountain, and our undefeated, nationally ranked football team was present to lay roses around the memorial.
>
> But there was a small potential to turn-off laced throughout the entire ceremony.
>
> As beautiful and well executed as it was, the entire production had a bit of a religious tone.
>
> Yes, religion and memorial go hand-in-hand, but the ceremony should not be treated like a funeral or a religious ceremony.
>
> Chaplain for the football team, Rev. Steve Harvey's speech, in its defense, represented more than just a religion connection. He brought attendees to the locker room with the team through his demonstration. It was not about praising a higher power to the majority of participants, but it was about a communal experience, all of us—fans, students, alumni and athletes—together as one.
>
> The prayer itself, however, was a less communal choice. Though not truly offensive, and easily understandable considering Harvey's relationship with the football team, a moment of silence, in which every person in attendance or watching the livestream could make his or her own decision as to how to pay tribute, would have been a more all-inclusive choice.
>
> The song Taylor Isaacs and Rodrigo Almeida performed so beautifully, "It Is Well With My Soul," also may have contributed to the ceremony's tendency to cross into unnecessarily religious territory. Though well meant, the lyrics of the song, particularly reference to Christian salvation as the source of all peace. True or not, the song suggests that there is there is only one way to peace after tragedy and creates a solemn environment rather than one that honors the lives of the 75.
>
> We, understandably, live in an area where ceremonies like the Memorial Ceremony all have a religious undertone. But at what

point do we decide the potential for turning people away because of religious affiliation overpowers the need to include it?

The Fountain Ceremony is one of the best moments in a son or daughter of Marshall's experience with the university. It is about coming together as one, and the sometimes overly religious nature of the ceremony threatens to take away from that—a sad reality in 21st century world in which we live.

It's not clear what the "sad reality" might be for this writer. That we've become so secular that people are offended at words of religious faith? That religious folks persist in being divisive? And is a hymn really "turning people away"? And if so, should that be sufficient cause for erasing a decades-long tradition, rooted in the original ceremony? Should prayers be excised? If not, might atheists be offended? And so we go down the rabbit hole.

Religion Notes: Odds and Ends

Throughout the era, *The Parthenon* and other university publications featured items that touched on faith, whether Christian or not:

- The 1976 yearbook featured a group photo of seventeen involved in the Word of Life Bible Study Rallies at the CCC. The national organization, headquartered in Schroon Lake, New York, was led by Jack Wyrtzen, who, like Billy Graham, was first involved in Youth for Christ. Strong on dispensationalism and biblical inerrancy, the Marshall group hosted eschatological-prophecy televangelist Jack Van Impe and a speaker from fundamentalist Hyles-Anderson College. They also sponsored a basketball team at Huntington City Mission.

- In that same yearbook, Josh McDowell, traveling representative for Campus Crusade for Christ and author of the popular (and still in print) apologetics book, *Evidence That Demands a Verdict* (1972), is shown speaking to a crowd at the Memorial Field House.

- In 1982, a memorial service was held for Salvadoran Catholic archbishop, Oscar Romero, who was assassinated in 1980 for his opposition to his government's military suppression (with U.S. funding) of "peasants" (his term) pressing for reform. The candlelight service included readings from Isaiah, Philippians, and Matthew; the singing of "Bridge Over Troubled Water" and "Kumbaya"; and readings from Romero's last sermon as well as a selection from the poetry of T. S. Eliot.

- A November 29, 1988 flyer distributed by the Muslim Students Association announced an evening's focus on the "Islamic Contribution to Civilization," including a session entitled "Palestinians: Blaming the Victims."

- The eighth annual CRU men's retreat focused on 1 Corinthians 16:13–14 (re standing firm in the faith). As one sophomore described these events, "Men from different backgrounds come together to learn more about God and biblical manhood, while creating new bonds with each other. One of the greatest things about the retreat is that we as men can be honest, vulnerable and show emotion, withholding nothing." (February 9, 2016)

- Vice President for Student Affairs, Cedric Gathings, when asked about his idea of "perfect happiness," said, "Perfect happiness is you just learning to accept things for how they are and just believing that God knows. Everything happens for a reason." (November 28, 2017)

- Herd4Christ, the campus Church of Christ group, was involved in a Christmas clothing giveaway, a practice in place for about ten years. (November 8, 2016).

- Members of "the Christian organization World Changers [SBC] volunteered at fourteen different worksites throughout the city," joining in such work with the over twelve thousand summer volunteers in fifty-one U.S. cities. (June 23, 2017)

- Valor Ministry, a new campus sub-group of Cru (formerly Campus Crusade for Christ), involved current and former military personnel in "in depth study of the Bible." (February 10, 2017)

- Two editorials deplored President Trump's 90-day ban on immigrants from Iran, Iraq, Libya, Somalia, Sudan, Syria, and Yemen, the first with the writer's recollection of her Muslim family's own immigration from Algeria, the second, by a Christian, quoting Leviticus 19:33–34 and Zechariah 7:10 on the proper treatment of foreigners. (January 31, 2017)

- In a guest column, Nigel Wallace urged Christians to "Practice Humility" (realizing "how important our own insignificance actually is"); to "Understand that Timing is Everything" (being patient with God's timing); and to "Give What You Need" (sharing love since you need it). (March 10, 2017)

- The Marshall Young Life group sent out leaders for local high school and middle school chapters. (March 14, 2017)

- Observing that "being a Muslim in America is so much scarier than what it should be," Karima Neghmouche urged readers to understand that "Allah means 'God.' The same God Christians and Jews worship . . . [and so, as she learned from her mother] "We're all going to the same place. We're just taking a different road there"; that "acts of crime in the name of Allah [are] the exact opposite of what Islam represents," for "Islam represents peace, charity, kindness, love and family" and "the radical acts that are committed are not by real Muslims." (July 8, 2016)

- MASS (Marshall Atheistic and Secular Society) was founded as "a place for atheists and skeptics, and just like any other campus group, [they] want to create a sense of community," in their case a place for "students who are non-religious or who are questioning their religious faith." (November 15, 2012)

- Mike Bartrum, a standout at tight end for Marshall, an all-pro long snapper for the Philadelphia Eagles, and grand-marshal of his alma mater's 2007 homecoming parade, had established "a Christian preschool for 42 kids on his farm in Pomeroy, Ohio, an hour north of Huntington" and was "working to establish Fellowship of Christian Athletes chapters in schools throughout the Tri-State Area." (*Marshall*, Spring, 2008)

- Michael W. Smith was recognized as a distinguished son of Marshall. As a Christian musician, he saw nine of his albums go gold and three platinum. He's also an author and record producer and has sung before presidents and with the Billy Graham Crusades. (*Marshall*, Spring 2010)

- Marshall held its first LGBTQ+ (Lesbian, Gay, Bisexual, Transgender, Queer/Questionning +) Lavender Graduation Ceremony, continuing "Marshall's tradition of pride and activism" and celebrating the academic achievements and contributions of the approximately twenty-five students expected to take part. President Gilbert was slated to deliver opening remarks, followed by the keynote by education professor Kathy Seelinger, and two staffers from the office of intercultural affairs. Each student would receive a lavender cord to wear at the university commencement. (Marshall University press release, April 23, 2018)

- Three LGBTQ+ groups were established by the office of multicultural affairs at Marshall—Queer to Slay (from a song lyric, meaning "queer and fabulous"), Trans-lation (self-explanatory), and Slaying Grace ("for students who are no longer welcome at their home churches or have lost their faith because of discrimination. Led by . . . [Presbyterian campus minister]Reverend Chris Bailey, it meets at the Campus Christian Center to provide an accepting church home on campus." (*Marshall* magazine, August, 2018)

And then there was this January 27, 2017 item in a special campus issue of *Herald-Dispatch*:

> The Episcopal Church welcomes you. Smart Theology & Fast Food. We're looking for: Students inspired by intelligent conversation about God and the world we live in, students unafraid of questions, students who enjoy conversation about spirituality. Join us each Sunday at 7PM in the Student Union ground floor for FREE food and smart discussion on spirituality.

A further word came from Greg Ganssle, who served as Campus Crusade director at Marshall from the fall of 1979 through the spring of 1983. (He also served as director at Yale for several years.) In his ministry, he found himself continually engaged with the work of philosophers, and the bug bit, leading him to earn a master's in philosophy at Rhode Island in 1990 and a doctorate from Syracuse in 1995. He's now a well-published professor of philosophy at Talbot Seminary.

He recalls particularly the work of Ed Tubbs, who, through the work of Navigators for over fifteen years, was "the anchor of evangelical ministry" on campus. (Tubbs went on to serve with Navigators in Russia and Estonia, and stateside at Ohio State and Kent State.) And then there's Chuck Fry, whose brother led Ganssle to Christ, and who has picked up the work of Navigators in Huntington.[93]

Ganssle also recalls the influence of two local pastors—Bob Massie of First Baptist Church, Ironton, just across the Ohio, and Gregg Terry, the same Gregg who wrote the letter of strong witness to *The Parthenon* back in the 1960s. Gregg's now emeritus pastor at Christ Community Church in Huntington, a church formed in the wake of the 1976, Campus Crusade for Christ campaign, "Here's Life, America." Ganssle remembers some resistance from the local churches, but the church plant took, and today it's a fixture in Huntington.[94] (Incidentally, Steve Harvey followed Bob Massie as associate pastor in Ironton, and now, as pastor of Ironton's Sharon Baptist Church, Harvey also serves as chaplain for the Marshall football team.)

Finally, in October 2013, on the roadside observation deck in Kenova, opposite the hill where the flight went down, an autographed ball signed and left by the women's soccer team offered up spirited slogans, such as "Go herd or go home," "Reach up and grab glory," and "Never forget." But the inscription by Kristine Culicerto #8 cited scripture: "I can do things through Him who strengthens me. Philippians 4:13." You don't have to look for long at Marshall to see the Word of God lifted up.

11

Three Spiritually-Impactful Pastors

THOUGH WE'VE FOCUSED ON campus affairs, local churches have had enormous impact on the Marshall University Community. Here are three pastors who've played key roles in this connection. Of course, this is simply a sampler, for many churches and pastors have served admirably and powerfully in discipling students. Some we've mentioned, but there are, of course, others.

Pastor R. F. Smith and Coaches Randle (1979–1983) and Pruett (1996–2004)

Coming to Huntington's Fifth Avenue Baptist Church in the late 1970s, Dr. R. F. Smith served around thirty years in that position, retiring in 1999 as Pastor Emeritus. Early on in Smith's ministry there, Marshall's football coach, Sonny Randle, turned to him for help, which might have seemed unlikely at first glance.

> Because Randle was divorced he was viewed as a playboy, which led to a mistaken image of him as a heavy drinker. Actually, he never touched alcohol. He attended church regularly and was never without a chaplain for his teams. His lone visible vice was betting on the horses, which he did quite well.[95]

Randle, who'd said he resign if he couldn't produce a winner, was at a very low point after the loss to Western Carolina in 1983. Coming into the game, the team was 1–3, and the 7–21 defeat before a homecoming crowd hit him particularly hard.

For advice, Randle sought the help of Dr. R. F. Smith senior minister at Fifth Avenue Baptist Church and the team's chaplain. Carrying a burden to Smith was not unusual for Randle. The coach had gone to his confidant for help with problems on and off the field since deciding he wanted Smith to be team chaplain. The decision was beneficial to both parties. Randle found the source of inspiration and Smith a means to fill the void in his life created by the death of his teenage son just a few months earlier. [A struggle Smith chronicled in his 1997 book, *Sit Down God . . . I'm Angry: A Grieving Father's Conversation with God.*] Smith however didn't accept the role unconditionally.

"We went out to lunch and I told him upfront that if he just wanted window dressing to look good in the religious community, I wasn't his man," Smith recalled. "I had to have a green ticket to minister to every ear—coaches and players. Sunny gave me a blank check. I had an open-door policy. I was included in executive sessions with coaches and the team. I felt free in their office and they felt free in mine. Now, Sonny and I had some head-to-head discussions, but regardless of disagreements we might have, he never reneged on his commitment to me from that first meeting." There were times, particularly early in Randle's tenure, when criticism of his coaching methods was prevalent, that Smith and Randle conversed almost daily. And not necessarily about football. "There were a lot of one-on-ones in those early days," Smith said. "We spent many hours in my library at home, secluded, talking not just about football, but life in general. Sonny became as close to me as a brother."

Nothing, however, had the impact on Randle and his program as did the meetings Smith conducted with the coach, his staff and players in the days after the loss to Western Carolina. The players voiced their concerns on the season to date, their individual performances, the job their coaches were doing and their hopes for the rest of the season. "I went in and jotted down on the back of an old program the list of their concerns," Smith said of the team meeting. "I assured them I would take the information to Sonny and the other coaches with no names attached. So many of the problems were simply tied to communication and a misunderstanding of the motives."

Randle had listened before and at times acted. But this time he took the concerns to heart. With various adjustments in the work he demanded from his players, both on and off the field, Randle depressurized the setting in which they had to perform. Practices, although still conducted under the same regimen, but without much contact, were more spirited almost immediately. "You could sense a world of difference in those first couple of days," Echols said. "It was like the Herd was a new team. It felt good to get ready to play, then great when Saturday came." [Wide receiver Bill] Hynus gave much of the credit to Smith. "I don't know what Dr. Smith did, but it made a world of difference in coach Randle the last part of that season. He changed off the field in practice and on the sidelines, and it really helped our team."

Smith insisted he performed no miracles. It was all a part of Randall's maturing process. A process that brought him more in touch with the changes football and society had undergone since he had entered coaching more than a decade before. "We had a long conversation about philosophy and some theology, and really what the whole business of leading people was all about," said Smith, himself a former athlete. "There are two schools of thought in coaching. One group coaches football and another coaches young men. And there is a decided difference in the two. Sonny started out coaching football, but in his later days, he moved his thinking to, 'These are men I'm coaching' and started to relate to them more in that light. One of the things that was key in the whole situation was that he was now dealing with a group of players who were products of a more permissive society."

"No longer was the military influence under which Sonny and I grew up in prevalent. It was 'Yes sir,' 'No sir,' a salute and do the job. It was no longer a groups of kids reared in the 50s and early 60s. The players were now questioning things. Slowly, Sonny grasped this and started implementing changes. To Sonny's credit, he moved 110 percent on those players' concerns."[96]

After the Western Carolina game, the Herd went 3–3, and it's said that "Dr. R. F. Smith was instrumental in Marshall's improved play late in the 1983 season." Still, it wasn't enough to save his job, but Randle, in a letter to the local paper "thanked the community for its support during his five years. He said he was a better person for the experience of trying to bring Marshall a winning program and had gained a new perspective on himself and football because of it."

Coach Pruett was a member at Fifth Avenue Baptist Church, where R. F. Smith was pastor. When Smith died, Pruett spoke movingly at his funeral. As Bob Hardwick, a Barboursville banker, remembers, "Coach Pruett cried uncontrollably while talking about his love and respect for his friend. Our coach laid open his heart for all to see."[97]

Smith's daughter, Rebecca, became a columnist, and at her site (rebeccafayesmithgalli.com), she posted an illustrated recording of one of her father's pastoral prayers:

> Holy Father, help us to hear you knocking at the doors of our soul. And may we answer and open our doors so you can come into our lives anew and afresh, even as you're coming to the world on the winds of spring that is clothing all nature in new garments. Ah, Father, your world's getting so beautiful. Almost hourly we see changes. Trees trimmed in green lights. Flowers beginning to strut their many colors. Foliage struggling for status. Dogwoods dividing between white and pink, and tulips cupping themselves for the freshness of your showers. O, Father, help us to so open our souls to the fresh showers of your blessings and opportunities and challenges and to open ourselves to the grace of your forgiveness. Forgive our foolish ways. Reclothe us in our rightful minds. May our sins be washed away as spring rains wash the debris of pruned nature, cleansing the earth for new growth. Grow within us O Lord. Wash us, cleanse us and fit us to live with you and ourselves and each other. Our world is still troubled, Lord. People are fighting and dying and running and scared. Please give leaders the insight to initiate peace. Grant wisdom that will find ways to peace and love and grace to all who are scared for their very lives. Many are scared today. Some scared of disease that threatens them. Some scared of job loss. Some scared of life and some scared of love and what it demands. Some scared because they are alone and lonely. O, Father, when all who this hour hurt and tremble with life's struggles, pour the healing balm of your love and grace and care. This we pray in the strong name of Jesus Christ. Amen.

Reggie Hill

Rising from the ashes of the plane crash, the football team grew in strength until they achieved an undefeated season (13–10) in 1999. Pastor Reggie Hill of Antioch Missionary Baptist Church provided spiritual background on a number of the key players on that team, e.g., captain Andre O'Neal, who was a testifier to his faith; who asked the coach, "Could we change the name of a play? It's derogatory to females"; and who went on to play for the Kansas City Chiefs, the Green Bay Packers, and the Minnesota Vikings. Then there was Paul Toviessi, who played for the Denver Broncos and who provided funding for the Paul & Robin Toviessi Nursery. Another door bears the sign, "Nate Ruffin & Sandra Barnett Education Room." (Ruffin missed the 1970 flight because of an injury, and he went on to captain the 1971 team.) Nate and Sandra were behind a scholarship program.

A series of plaques on the fellowship hall wall, assembled under the heading "Go Ye Therefore and Teach All Nations . . . Matthew 28:19," features photos of over twenty families who've moved to other locales, carrying the gospel preached at Antioch. Some are athletic luminaries, e.g., Chris Parker (a running back who played for the Jacksonville Jaguars) and Dwight Freeman (who'd been head basketball coach at Marshall). Also displayed is a newspaper article about a "lucky" T-shirt Girardi Mercer wore in Marshall's Motor City Bowl game. He'd worn it since high schools days, in almost a hundred games, and it was pretty ragged. His mother bought it for him at a Baptist conference in New Orleans, with the wording, "Hooked on Jesus."

The list goes on, for Reggie's memory (and the memory of his wife Josette) is rich in detail. For instance, he recalls a player who came to their home for Bible study and another who made it to church each Sunday.[98]

An article in the Fall 2019 issue of *Marshall Magazine* honors another Marshall athlete, who made her mark outside of sports. As VP for human resources at Roche, the world's largest biotech company, Cindy Carlisle, who was a track star at Marshall, was recognized, along with Oprah Winfrey and Serena Williams, as one of the most influential women of color in corporate America. She recalls,

> My church friends at Antioch Baptist church became an extended family. They would pick me up every Sunday from my dorm and take me to church. When I came back to visit Marshall about 10 years after I graduated, the church bus driver recognized me at a football game and remembered picking me up at Holderby Hall. He was genuinely happy to see me come back to visit.

Adam Goodwin

One of the students converted in the 1990s has proven to be a key player in the spiritual life of Marshall in the following decades. When he arrived on campus in 1997, he was lost. He'd walk by the Christian Center and would feel no affinity for the activities therein. But a fellow student, who was the son of American Baptist student worker, Jerry Losh, asked him if he were a Christian and then invited him to attend a Baptist Collegiate Ministry meeting, which ran about one hundred twenty five students. (The two were subsequently on annual training with the Army Reserves the summer of 1998, and when Adam returned, he plugged in and was converted.)

Goodwin flourished in BCM, graduating from Marshall in 2002. Sensing a call to ministry, he headed to Southeastern Baptist Theological Seminary in Wake Forest, North Carolina, where he received the MDiv in 2005. From there, he headed to the College of Charleston in the West Virginia capital, where he served on the BCM staff until he returned as Losh's successor in 2008. Back in Huntington, he joined with the Marshall Community Fellowship and became a lay elder. (It was an ABC church founded by Kenova Baptist Church, but both KBC and MCF have now joined the SBC.) When MCF's founding pastor left in 2014, the church, made up largely of Marshall students, asked Adam to fill the pulpit, and then to become the pastor in 2015. At this point, he stepped down from his official ministry position at Marshall. In those days, the congregation met above Latta's office supply store, a block west of the campus, but then moved to a warehouse a few blocks south of the football stadium, space they converted for use in worship, fellowship, and child care.

Though he no longer holds an office in the CCC, his ministry to students is deep and extensive. Their testimonies and demonstrations of growth and teamship within this fellowship are gratifying. Over a hundred attend a Tuesday night service and enjoy a good measure of discipleship, including substantial involvement in ministry, with a number serving on the church missions committee.

Reflecting on trends, Goodwin sees a spiritual hunger on campus, with curiosity regarding truth, but it's not so Christianly directed; he and his staff (with key ones from his former BCM group at Marshall) are finding anxiety and depression growing among the students, much of it coming from not getting enough "likes" on Facebook. Along the way, he's become increasingly convinced that the local church is the key to campus ministry.

As for the CCC and its temper, he says it's an ever-changing thing as students and ministers and ministries move in and out. It's all very fluid as classes graduate, new personalities show up to direct the denominations' work, funding surges and falls away in first one place and then another. (When low attendance makes CCC rent and the cost of a staffer unfeasible, then offices will shut down, as was the case with the Episcopal work.) And there have been instances when an open office was rented to a local church for a campus base of ministry. Again, very fluid, with the individual ministries and the CCC collectively taking on the character of whoever is involved and in charge at the moment.[99]

12

The Spiritual Future?

It's fascinating to track the life of schools that started with Christian orientation: Some still bear the label 'Christian' (or a specific denominational label) but have long since abandoned the core doctrines. Rather, they speak of a religious heritage or spiritual values or some such. Of course, some have stayed faithful to those beginnings, either through constancy or through periodic upheavals of renewal. Marshall, unlike others with founding doctrinal allegiances, became a state school in the nineteenth century of its founding. While such Methodist schools as Northwestern and Vanderbilt stayed private as they shed their scriptural focus, Marshall, like Rutgers, began with specifically Christian purposes, but then became a public institution. (For instance, Rutgers was chartered as Queen's College, established to "educate the youth in language, liberal, the divinity, and useful arts and sciences," the "the divinity" specifically that which was recognized by the Dutch Reformed Church, whose ministers the school was designed to train.)

University to Multiversity to Monoversity

Historically, one might say, the *university* has morphed into the *multiversity*, and now into the *monoversity*. Originally, as in the case of Harvard, America's oldest university, there was a religious core that held everything in that particular academic *universe* together. It was reflected in its seventeenth century seal, which included "Christo" and "Ecclesiae" along with "Veritas." Today, that tradition lives on in such colleges as Wheaton, whose motto is "For Christ and His Kingdom," and whose faculty—from physicists to philosophers to sociologists to artists—are required to take a course on the "integration of faith and learning," persuaded that "all truth is God's truth" and that the Bible is bedrock truth.

Typically, the universities' integrating core disintegrated, as indifference or hostility toward Scripture arose and as doctoral programs (famously in the German universities) rewarded narrow specialization throughout an increasing number of disciplines, producing the "silo effect" of the *multiversity*. The main shared values were academic freedom, scientism, and the belief that their untrammeled exercise was a boon to human progress. In spiritual terms, it was a laissez faire enterprise.

From the latter part of the twentieth century, a new sort of "higher education" institution has emerged, one in which uniformity of thought and action is not only manifested but enforced—the *monoversity*. The live-and-let-live ethos is being displaced by new orthodoxies, but not the original ones tied to biblical theology. Rather, they're based on psychosocial trends with their own pieties to be observed, rituals to be performed, and heresies to be rooted out and punished.

One might have thought the universities would have turned to a secular value core, such as natural law, as found in the writings of Aristotle, Cicero, Aquinas, Averroes, Grotius, Locke, and Lao-Tzu—something compatible with the schools' Christian roots, but not sectarian. Unfortunately, this was still too narrow. Instead, "feelings" and "diversity" have become the core values, which is to say there is no core value at all, for these are infinitely subjective, malleable, and even grotesque. Or, to use the old imagery of the prophet Amos, there is no plumb line to hang beside the wall to see if it stands straight.

Of course, the authorities give tacit assent to this problem when, in practice, they disallow certain "feelings" (of racial hatred) and suppress certain forms of "diversity" (young-earth creationism) on their faculty. But it's hard for them to say why exactly these are out of bounds without appealing to standards of value which they have themselves undercut. It just becomes arbitrary.

Intellectual Dead Ends

In his 1987 book, *The Closing of the American Mind*, University of Chicago Professor Allan Bloom offered one take on the highest good in the modern university—tolerance or openness. While it used to be the case that such virtues as honesty and industry determined who was honored on campus, these now amounted to nothing if the possessor was perceived to lack tolerance/respect for whatever else showed up (perceived intolerance excepted). One could be a plagiarizing slacker and still enjoy good campus status if only he signaled that he was okay with what others were up to. No moral judgment or rebuke. No suggestion that *their own* truth might not be *the* truth, or that there was such a thing as *the* truth in the realm of metaphysics and ethics. To dissent from this conceit could disqualify the speaker for respect and social viability on campus.

Today's version of Bloom's blunt instrument is "sensitivity," the watchword of those complaining that they are unfairly marginalized, threatened, alienated, triggered, unsafe, etc. It seeks out unintentional "microaggressions" in the absence of conscious, serious aggression or offense (micro or macro). And it generalizes from upsetting anecdotes to sweeping traumas.

Of course, fellow-feeling and compassion are Christian virtues, but they are not absolutes. As is well demonstrated before our very eyes throughout the culture, obsessive attendance to hurt feelings is the universal solvent, washing away any possibility of taking a reasonable stand for or against a position. It puts a weapon of mass destruction in the hands of those who insist on having their way, however flawed their thinking and behavior might be. Claim that you are wounded, traumatized, appalled, or whatever distress word works best, and the argument is over, especially if you can deploy a word of utter cancellation, e.g., the dismissive branding of "phobes" or "racists."

Of course, this strikes at the very heart of the academic enterprise, but it elevates at least two classic fallacies to sainthood—*ad misericordiam* (appeal to pity) and *ad hominem* (attacking the person rather than their argument). And it short circuits the classic form of argument, *reductio ad absurdum* (reduction to absurdity), the technique Socrates modeled to get at the essence of things and the truth of matters. It works when the parties take turns proposing different concepts, principles, and explanations, which then may be scrutinized "hammer and tongs." If an idea proves to be bogus, its implications and applications absurd, then its advocate has to junk it or try a tweak for another go. But when we lose our ability to recognize or admit absurdity when it actually occurs, but rather take offense at the mere suggestion that we've blown it, then "game over." Actually, academia over. Thankfully, in science (where it's called the hypothetico-deductive method), they're more inclined to honor it, especially in the "hard sciences" such as physics and chemistry. In the social sciences and the humanities, the picture is not so rosy. The search for reasonableness often disintegrates into functional relativism, where power rather than truth is the aim. And it's pretty much anything goes discursively—post-modernism, if you will, which flourishes on the modern university campus.

A Strange Inversion

A strange inversion occurs: Whereas once traditional (indeed, ancient) Christian convictions were platformed and "infidels" tolerated, now "infidels" are platformed and those with traditional Christian convictions are merely tolerated. That is, until they're not. For there comes a time when plain biblical speaking on these matters becomes so "offensive," so damaging to feelings and "unity," that it is proscribed as "hate speech."

How does Christian ministry continue on campus under these circumstances? The most obvious route is by avoiding certain clear teachings of the Bible, by watering down its descriptions and prescriptions, or by twisting its message to avoid confrontation. Some do this naturally as they've slipped into a more Schleiermachean mode, making sure their deliverances are acceptable to the church's "cultured despisers" (cf. the 1799 give-away-the-store effort of Friedrich Schleiermacher to ingratiate Christianity to its critics). But there does come a time when it's fair to ask if the Christianity they purvey is any longer the real thing.

How do things get this way? It takes a cooperative effort spanning decades. Among the typical players and forces are university staff and students who see to it that, or fail to object when, faculty inimical to the founders' best dreams are hired; new trustees either keen on or indifferent to such change; pursuit of funding, students, accreditation, and acclaim driving the administration to check off boxes they would otherwise ignore or denounce; athletic programs indulgent toward wayward players who make a mockery of the school's traditional values; students marinated in unseemly and toxic social agendas who are, nevertheless, granted platforms and programs beyond their wisdom; leaders who fear that the school will suffer a public relations disaster if it doesn't toe the societal line (or like Hollywood, toe the guild line, society be damned).

The end result is that state schools become indifferent to the fact that they take taxpayer money to undermine the faith and values of its constituency, even when that faith and those values are sound. Of course, this doesn't limit the religious freedom of students to grow in faith. Indeed, faith often flourishes in persecution. And there are vital churches to give them succor. But again, why should those churches subsidize institutions directed at countervailing the venerable message they preach and teach, the message that grounded that very institution?

What might this "religion" be that displaces Christianity at the heart of the school? Is it it pluralism (a sort of westernized version of the Baha'i faith)? Hedonism? Therapeutic deism? Nihilism? Utilitarianism? Something has to fill the void.

Of course, diversity is treated unreflectively as an unalloyed good, undergirding "unity in diversity" which is "our greatest strength." In practice, it means "our kind of diversity," "diversity we think is kosher or innocuous," or "diversity which offends people we'd like to see offended." It doesn't translate into greater representation of avowed evangelicals on the faculty or into a "True Love Waits"(chastity till marriage) columnist in the paper. The dismissive narrative holds that the Judeo-Christian-Western tradition is hegemonic and oppressive, and that the only diversity needing celebration is dissent from that hegemony. But this conceit ignores the fact that the campus "cancel culture" at public universities is not the brain child of "Bible thumpers."

In Marshall's case, the question is particularly keen because the school rests in the traditional Bible Belt. That very fact has slowed the disintegration of genuine (as opposed to domesticated or mutilated) Christianity. But it has also generated a secular crusading spirt in some key players who've shaped the school, powerful figures who've taken it upon themselves to "liberate" students from their "backward" surroundings. And so the struggle continues.

The Leprous Charley Ward

In the spring of 2001, Heisman Trophy winner and New York Knicks star, Charley Ward, had the temerity to try to lead a Jewish *New York Times* reporter, Eric Konigsberg, to Christ. Eric ("E" as they called him) was visiting a Bible study attended by Ward and his teammate Allan Houston. In the course of the gathering, Ward told "E" that accepting Jesus as Savior and Lord was essential to a right relationship with God.

Hearing this, *Chicago Tribune* sportswriter, Melissa Isaacson, herself Jewish, went off on Ward, identifying him with those who "babble words of hate and nonsense" and tossing in expressions like "racist" and "insidious brand of bigot." Her *Tribune* colleague Skip Bayless rose to Ward's defense, saying that his words, however clumsy, were taken out of context, and that sharing one's biblical faith was just what Christians did.

Bayless's column was as mild-mannered as Isaacson's was not, and what he said seemed not only gracious but obvious. So it was surprising to read a follow-up piece by the paper's ombudsman, Don Wycliff, calling Bayless's piece "one of the most courageous newspaper columns I've seen in years." It hardly seemed heroic, but that's where things have landed—and this was two decades ago. Today, the cancel culture has shifted into high gear. Thus anyone suggesting that hell is real and that escape from it and hope of heaven depend upon accepting by faith the atoning death of God's Son on the cross, is ripe for social oblivion. And, of course, this dynamic extends beyond journalism into academia.

Whither Marshall?

A century ago, according to the Marshall yearbook, graduating senior Charles Bennet Halstead of Hunt, West Virginia, "when very young . . . formulated a theory of evolution which he afterwards found to coincide with that of Darwin. He has ideas of his own about religion. Although not a woman hater he takes more pleasure in delving into nature's history than into the unexplored regions where the tyrant King Cupid reigns." The Scopes Trial was still a decade away, and Halstead was definitely "out there" in his religious convictions. But he was tolerated by those whose "ideas about religion" were of the more orthodox persuasion.

As noted earlier, the Campus Crusade students, under the direction of political science professor Melvin Miller, delivered their message publicly in front of the campus clock in the late 1960s. And in the years following the crash, the annual Memorial Fountain observances were replete with Christian input and themes. You might say that the Marshall tradition has been that Christian perspectives were platformed and non-Christian, sub-Christian, and anti-Christian perspectives were tolerated.

With the publication of sexually-illicit advice columns in *The Parthenon* and the characterization of visiting campus preachers as "extremists," needing to be tolerated, it appears that the flip is under way. Perhaps these examples were outliers, lonely anecdotes signifying little. But it may well be the case that they are telling, indicating that the Bible is more indulged than honored, with the heterodox and peculiar more obviously celebrated. Still, happy to say, there seems to be room for both. But can this hold?

Credit is due to President Gilbert for standing up for the rights of "extreme persons" to speak an edgy word of biblical counsel to students who may choose to walk on by if they find it offensive. This is consistent with what we read in a Marshall Magazine article (Autumn, 2018) on the diversity initiative by the Marshall office of multicultural affairs. Therein, Dr. Gilbert is quoted, "My goal is for Marshall University to be a place free from all forms of discrimination, a place where all people feel welcome and all opinions are respected."

This approximates classic liberal sentiment—reciprocal hearings in the free market place of ideas. But, of course, it is not absolutely true (nor should it be) that there should be *no* forms of discrimination in a place where *all* people feel welcome and *all* opinions respected. Seriously, should neo-Nazis be supplied a meeting room and granted respect, rather than disparagement, for their public commendation of *The Protocols of the Elders of Zion*? And what if an advocacy group (analogous to the campus suffragettes of the early twentieth century) urged the repeal of anti-bestiality laws? Should they be given space for their cause in *The Parthenon*? The simple point is that any school with a lick of sense and a discernible spine will draw lines on what is appallingly outlandish.

The concern then is whether what was once appallingly outlandish, especially in the sexual realm, is displacing what was once winsomely obvious—and whether discrimination and dishonor now fall upon those whose roots are traditionally intertwined with Marshall's.

Of course, even if the words of the Bible (responsibly interpreted and not twisted to accommodate whatever the culture might prefer at the moment) are shunned or mocked at Marshall, God will still do his work on campus and in the churches. The question is whether the school will treasure the counsel of the Bible or find it noxious. If treasured, then surely offense and division could occur, for the Bible is a book with edge. But when was edge anathema in the university?

After a beginning with "old-time religion," the school has seen the emergence and re-emergence at various times of "new-time religion" (Jennings), "new-time irreligion" (SDS, atheist club), and "new old-time religion" (Melvin Miller and Crusade)—with various admixtures of the three. Will there be a place for each as the school goes forward? Surveying the national university scene today, the prospects are not promising. But Marshall can be the exception, to the applause of its founders and curators through its first century and beyond.

"A Relentless Quest for Truth"

Back in the 1960s, President Stewart Smith issued a statement prompted by the state board of education's vote to permit the sale of beer on campuses under their purview and a poll of Marshall students showing 2:1 support for the policy change. Smith had also been flooded with letters, calls, and petitions of alarm from "parents, alumni, friends and businessmen"—as many as seven hundred "communications on the subject." In response, he declared that there would be no such sales at that time. He noted that beer was quite available nearby in the city, and he expressed concern that "convivial frivolities" might distract students from their studies. Framing the decision was his opening sentence: "Our purpose at Marshall University is a relentless quest for truth, and our goal is to prepare students for a better way of life."

A noble sentiment, yet one with precious little respect on the modern university campus. The "relentless quest for truth" is actually quite terrifying, even repugnant. For one thing, it assumes that there is such a thing as *the* truth, a notion that's an affront to those who insist there is only *my* truth and *your* truth, to people who are keen to "deconstruct" texts that espouse universal verities, counting them oppressive. And the same goes for the concept of "a better way of life," for who's to say that your lifestyle choices are better (or worse) than mine? Again, who are you to legislate morality for others or to say that this path rather than that one leads to human flourishing? It's all relative.

As for the "relentless quest," it's hardly so when those with well-engineered grumps can scuttle discourse. And so the university retreats to something more along the lines of devotion to "a relentless quest for dumbing down discussion, lest purveyors of nonsense, misdirection, and disinformation be held accountable for their errors." Or perhaps, "a relentless quest for optimum branding in a culture gone mad."

Marshall is well and widely celebrated for its rise "from ashes to glory" in athletics. It may be positioned because of its history and setting to exhibit another sort of campus glory that could inspire beleaguered schools throughout the land, schools longing (perhaps secretly) for the day when their institutions might be intoxicated, not with social fear and posturing, but rather with "a relentless quest for truth."

The Last Word

Not the writer's last word on the spiritual history of Marshall, but the literal last word on the course of world history. Whatever the future of Marshall (or any university) might be, in the end, all involved will have to admit that Christ is king, many with gladness, many with regret. Those who've been devoted to his gospel and his teachings will be vindicated; those who've ignored, dismissed, or disparaged the Bible will be embarrassed. And through it all, God is sovereign over all, his will unperturbed by the counsel of gainsayers. Most importantly, his grace and transforming love is ever available to those who turn to him in repentance and faith. It's that simple. It's that inevitable. So we close with this poetic declaration from Philippians 4:5–11 (HCSB) to put the whole affair in perspective:

> In your relationships with one another, have the same mindset as Christ Jesus:
>
> Who, being in very nature God,
> did not consider equality with God something
> to be used to his own advantage;
> rather, he made himself nothing
> by taking the very nature of a servant,
> being made in human likeness.
> And being found in appearance as a man,
> he humbled himself
> by becoming obedient to death—
> even death on a cross!
> Therefore God exalted him to the highest place
> and gave him the name that is above every name,
> that at the name of Jesus every knee should bow,
> in heaven and on earth and under the earth,
> and every tongue acknowledge that Jesus Christ is Lord,
> to the glory of God the Father.

Appendix

Principals and Presidents

In 2013, Lisle G. Brown (curator of special collections at Marshall for forty years) wrote a research piece entitled *Principles and presidents of Marshall University: 1837–2013*.[100] In it he noted religious connections for the various leaders, and here is a selection of items he covered. No doubt other principals and presidents were involved in churches, but Brown found these linkages noteworthy. (He also wrote extensively on Mormon history, and had earned an MA in history and religious studies from Marshall.)

Principals of Marshall Academy, 1837–1867

Jacob Harris Patton (1839–1840): licensed to preach by the presbytery of New York, and author of *A Popular History of the Presbyterian Church in the United States* (1901) and *Which Religion Satisfies the Wants of the Soul?*

Alfred E. Thom (1840–843): a graduate of Presbyterian Theological Seminary, who served as pastor of the Western Church in Guyandotte and later of Huntsville (TX) Presbyterian Church

Josiah Baird Poage (1843–1850): a Presbyterian minister who graduated from Princeton Seminary and who succeeded Alfred Thom as pastor of Western Church, having served in Presbyterian offices in the East before coming to Marshall; and who, in points west after leaving Marshall, was "emphatically a Christian gentleman, decided in his opinions, but charitable in his spirit"

William B. McFarland (1850–853): who, having switched from the Presbyterian to the Methodist faith when he was nineteen, was a Methodist Episcopal pastor, not only in Huntington, but also in Missouri

Staunton V. Field (1853–1854): a Methodist Episcopal minister who had pastored in Suffolk, Virginia

William R. Boyers (1854–1858): a Presbyterian entrusted with leadership of a school belonging to the Methodist Episcopal Conference

Daniel Webster Thrush (1861): licensed (but not ordained) to preach in the Lutheran Church, a teacher at Young Ladies Seminary in Augusta, KY, before coming to Marshall

Principals of Marshall College, 1867–1896

James Beauchamp Clark (1873–1874): a self-declared "Campbellite [Church of Christ/Restorationist] in religion" in his original application to the college

William Joseph Kenny, Sr. (1884–1886): an Irishman who, before leaving the Catholic priesthood, served parishes in California

Thomas Edward Hodges (1886–1896): according to West Virginia state treasurer Merrill Carrico (at the dedication of Hodges Hall in 1937), "an Elder in the Presbyterian Church for more than twenty-five years and . . . a member of its College Board for the United States"

Presidents of Marshall College, 1896–1946

Lawrence Jugurtha Corbly (1896–1907 as principal; 1907–1915 as president): one known for "excelling as a teacher of science, the languages and the Bible," who preached as a substitute at Huntington's Central Christian Church on the morning of his death

Morris Purdy Shawkey (1923–1935): a professor at Methodist schools before (at West Virginia Wesleyan) and after (at Morris Harvey, now U. of Charleston) his time at Marshall

James Edward Allen (1935–1942): Professor Emeritus upon his retirement from Marshall, who'd come to the school after twenty-five years as president of the Presbyterian College, Davis and Elkins, and had found "the secular atmosphere at Marshall quite 'alien'"

Presidents of Marshall University, 1946–2013

John Grove Barker (1971–1974): a Presbyterian elder who penned a number of memorable prayers

Robert Bruce Hayes (1974–1983): a one-time dean of Marshall teachers college, who also taught at such Christian schools as Taylor (non-denominational, with Methodist roots), Asbury (Wesleyan-Holiness), and Warner Southern (Church of God, Anderson)

Dale Frederick Nitzschke (1984–1990) a graduate of the Catholic Loras College, where he once served as instructor

Endnotes

1. Moffat, *Marshall University*, 13.
2. Neuhaus, *The Naked Public Square*.
3. Brown, "Principals and presidents," 32, 27.
4. Moffatt, *Marshall University*, 29.
5. Moffatt, *Marshall University*, 34.
6. *Service With Fighting Men*, 298.
7. *Service With Fighting Men*, 312–13.
8. *Service With Fighting Men*, 313.
9. Moffat, *Marshall University*, 29.
10. Larmer, *Operation Yao Ming*, 5.
11. Larmer, *Operation Yao Ming*, 6.
12. Larmer, *Operation Yao Ming*, 6–7.
13. Moffat, *Marshall University*, 28.
14. Moffat, *Marshall University*, 42.
15. Horner, "Kanamori, 353.
16. Moffat, *Marshall University*, 67.
17. Moffat, *Marshall University*, 61–2.
18. Moffat, *Marshall University*, 51.
19. Moffat, *Marshall University*, 63.
20. Moffat, *Marshall University*, 63.
21. Moffat, *Marshall University*, 64–65.
22. Moffat, *Marshall University*, 94.
23. "One Hundred Years."
24. Brown, "Principals and presidents," 32, 49.
25. Brown, "Principals and presidents," 59–64.
26. Massey, "The 1940s."
27. Massey, "The 1940s."
28. "Analysis of Unpaid (Regular) Pledges."
29. For instance, a March 25, 1966, letter to President Smith notes contributions pledged or paid from INCO (International Nickel Company), Twentieth Street Bank, Boone County Coal Company, and J. P. Hamer Lumber Company.
30. Moffat, *Marshall University*, 200.
31. Moffat, *Marshall University*, 170.
32. Moffat, *Marshall University*, 170.
33. Moffat, *Marshall University*, 159.

34. "motive Magazine."

35. *motive*, "Questions?"

36. Conversation with Bos and Dottie Johnson, Woodlands Retirement Community, Huntington, October 18, 2014.

37. Schulman, *The Seventies*, xii, xvi-xvii.

38. Burkirk, "Mood of the Campus."

39. Boyd, *Are Your Running?* 5, 8, 12, 14.

40. Boyd, *Are You Running?* 89.

41. Slaatte, *The Dogma*, 95.

42. Slaatte, *Time, Existence, and Destiny,* 86.

43. Slaatte, *Discovering*, 69.

44. Slaatte, *Discovering*, 63-4.

45. Slaatte, *Discovering*, 11-7, 19-24, 45-51.

46. Slaatte, *Discovering*, 39-40.

47. Slaatte, *Discovering*, 57-9.

48. Moffatt, *Marshall University*, 140.

49. Slaatte, "A Personal Perspective."

50. Jennings, *Bibliography & Biography*, v.

51. Jennings, *Bibliography & Biography*, 35.

52. Case, *Jesus: A New Biography* 356-7, 371, 440.

53. Moffat, *Marshall University*, 159.

54. Jennings, *Function*, 80.

55. Jennings, *Function*, 126.

56. Jennings, *Function*, 127.

57. Jennings, *Function*, 86-8.

58. Williams, *Trousered Apes*, 78.

59. Williams, *Trousered Apes*, 32-3.

60. Williams, *Trousered Apes*, 113.

61. Williams, *To Be*, 50.

62. Williams, *Trousered Apes*, 129-30.

63. Williams, *Trousered Apes*, back-cover blurb.

64. Hennen, "Struggle for Recognition."

65. Conversation with Alan Wild, Huntington, May 20, 2013.

66. Wilson, "Collection 515."

67. Greenlee, *November Ever After,* 32-3.

68. *For All Time* and *Real Tragedy.*

69. Phone conversation with Phil Wilks, August 6, 2016.

70. Louisville conversation with Kris Wilks, August 6, 2016. She also recalls that Herndon Wilks, 92-years old in 2005, was the oldest living Marshall player at the time. Kris's brother Phil also played for Marshall, and later distinguished himself through fifteen years of coaching at Maryville College in Tennessee, where his record in turning around the program earned him a place on the school's wall of fame. Her brother, Roger, also played at Marshall, and his son, Scott, another member of the Thundering Herd went on to be a strength and conditioning coach for the University of Louisville football team.

71. Conversation with Andrew Earles, Marshall, Huntington, January 12, 2017.

72. Conversation with Bos and Dottie Johnson.

73. Conversation with C. E. Wilson, Huntington, December 3, 2014.

74. Telephone conversation with Bobby Bowden, June 29, 2020.

75. *Real Tragedy, Read Triumph*, 38–9.

76. "1970 Marshall Player."

77. *Ashes to Glory*.

78. Dawson, *Coach in progress*, 104–5.

79. Conversation with Dwain Gregory, NYC, May 8, 2014.

80. Conversation with Jim, Fugate, St. Albans, WV, October 7, 2013.

81. Conversation with Jim Howerton, Huntington, October 6, 2013.

82. "Chastened Chaplain."

83. Vecsey, "Fellowship of Christian Athletes."

84. Conversation with Syd Wheeler, Barboursville, WV, December 13, 2014.

85. Newquist, "Biography."

86. Conversation with Bob Bondurant, Barboursville, WV, December 3, 2014.

87. Chastain, *Purpose*, 82.

88. Chastain, *Purpose*, 118.

89. Chastain, *Purpose*, 232–33.

90. Chastain, *Purpose*, 233.

91. "Former NFL quarterback."

92. Perry, *The Declaration of Independence*, 267.

93. Conversation with Greg Ganssle, Evangelical Theological Society, Providence, Rhode Island, November, 2017.

94. Howard Snyder described it as "a multimillion-dollar evangelistic effort sponsored by Campus Crusade for Christ, localized in 253 U.S. metropolitan areas. It involved over 14,500 local churches, and three-fourths of all Americans were said to have been exposed to the campaign's catchy 'I Found It' slogan during the campaign."

95. Nolte, "Setting the Table," 64.

96. Nolte, "Setting the Table," 76–8.

97. Chastain, *Purpose*, 302–3.

98. Conversation with Reggie and Josette Hill, Huntington, July 25, 2016.

99. Phone conversation with Adam Goodwin, July 3, 2020.

100. Brown, "Principals and presidents."

Bibliography

Here is a selection of "external" sources (i.e., not published by Marshall). The exceptions are Lisle Brown's annotated roll call of the school's leadership through the decades and Charles Moffatt's substantial history of the university, published by the Alumni Association.

We should also note that the Bible is referenced and quoted frequently, though particular passages are not cited in the endnotes or bibliography. Suffice it to say that selections from the following books appear in the text: Genesis, Leviticus, Psalms, Ecclesiastes, Zechariah, Matthew, Mark, Luke, John, Acts, Romans, 1 Corinthians, 2 Corinthians, Galatians, Philippians, 1 John, James, and Revelation.

"1970 Marshall Player: Spared for a Reason." *Bethune-Cookman Wildcats* (February 19, 2014). https://bcuathletics.com/news/2014/2/19/1970_marshall_player_spared_for_a_reason.aspx.

Bloom, Allan. *The Closing of the American Mind: How Higher Education Has Failed Democracy and Impoverished the Souls of Today's Students.* New York: Simon & Schuster, 1987.

Boyd, Malcolm. *Are You Running With Me, Jesus? Prayers by Malcolm Boyd—Fortieth Anniversary Edition of the Spiritual Classic.* Cambridge Massachusetts: Cowley, 2006.

Brown, Lisle G. "Principals and Presidents of Marshall University, 1837–2013." Librarian Research: *Marshall Digital Scholar* (2013). https://mds.marshall.edu/lib_faculty/32/.

Case, Shirley Jackson. *Jesus: A New Biography.* Piscataway, New Jersey: Gorgias, 2006.

Chastain, *Purpose and Passion: Bobby Pruett & the Marshall Years.* Huntington: Mid-Atlantic Highlands, 2005.

"Chastened Chaplain: A Forthright Account of Failure and Renewal." Interview in Nashville: *SBC LIFE* (November 1, 2000).

Dawson, Red, with Patrick Garbin. *A Coach in Progress: Marshall Football—A Story of Survival and Revival.* New York: Sports Publishing, 2005.

For All Time: Marshall University's rise to a football powerhouse from the ashes of America's worst sports tragedy. The Herald-Dispatch, 2000.

Gay, Peter. *Modernism: The Lure of Heresy, from Baudelaire to Beckett and Beyond.* New York: W. W. Norton, 2010.

Bibliography

Greenlee, Craig T. *November Ever After: A memoir of tragedy and triumph in the wake of the 1970 Marshall football plane crash*. Bloomington, Indiana: iUniverse, 2011.

Hennen, John. "Struggle for Recognition: The Marshall University Students for a Democrtic Society and the Red Scare in Huntington, 1965–1969." *West Virginia History*, vol. 52 (1993). http://www.wvculture.org/history/journal_wvh/wvh52–59.html

Horner, Norman. "Kanamori, Tsurin ("Paul")." In *Biographical Dictionary of Christian Missions*. Grand Rapids: Eerdmans, 1997.

Jennings, Louis B. *The Bibliography & Biography of Shirley Jackson Case*. Chicago: University of Chicago, 1949.

———. *The Function of Religion: An Introduction* (Lanham, Maryland: University Press of America, 1979.

Larmer, Brook. *Operation Yao Ming: The Chinese Sports Empire, American Big Business, and the Making of an NBA Superstar*. New York: Botham, 2005.

Marshall University, Ashes to Glory: The Greatest Comeback Story in Sports History. Video by West Virginia Public Broadcasting (2006).

Massey, Tim R. "The 1940s: World War II dominated the decade." *The Herald-Dispatch* (June 12, 1999).

Moffat, Charles Hill. *Marshall University: A University Comes of Age, 1837–1980*. Huntington: Marshall University Alumni Association, 1981.

Neuhaus, Richard John. *The Naked Public Square: Religion and Democracy in America*, 2nd ed. Grand Rapids: Eerdmans, 1998.

Newquist, Gusti Linnea. "A Biography in Her Own Words." Shepherdstown Presbyterian Church. http://shepherdstownpresbyterian.org/news-media/news/spc-calls-reverend-gusti-linnea-newquist

Nolte, Rick. "Setting the Table: The Randle Years." *Rolling Thunder: Marshall University football, 1967–1987*. Huntington: RMR Books, 1989.

Pennington, Chad. "Former NFL quarterback Chad Pennington shares his story of sports and faith." *Sports Spectrum* video. https://www.youtube.com/watch?v=scjn_rZUfTM.

Perry, Simon D. *The Declaration of Independence, God, and Evolution*. Big Fork, 2016.

Real Tragedy, Real Triumph: True Stories and Images from the Crash and Rebirth of Marshall University Football. *The Herald-Dispatch*, 2006.

Schulman, Bruce J. *The Seventies: The Great Shift in American Culture, Society, and Politics*. Cambridge, Massachusetts: DaCapo, 2001.

Service With Fighting Men: An Account of the Work of the American Young Men's Christian Association in the World War, vol. 1. New York: Association Press, 1922.

Slaatte, Howard A. *Discovering Your Real Self: Sermons of Existential Relevance*. Lanham, Maryland: University Press of America, 1980.

———."A Personal Perspective of Plott and His Plottings." Paper read at the 1995 International Society of the Comparative Study of Civilizations. http://www.sckans.edu/~gray/plott16.html

Smith, R. F. Smith, Jr. *Sit Down, God . . . I'm Angry: A Grieving Father's Conversation with God*. Valley Forge: Judson, 1997.

Utterback, William Irvin. *The Great Life Cycle: an Illustrated Presentation of the past, Present and Future on the Bases of Scripture*. Huntington: Gentry Brothers, 1927.

Vecsey, George. "The Fellowship of Christian Athletes: A Love Cult That Continues to Grow." *New York Times* (August 22, 2020). https://www.nytimes.com/1971/08/22/archives/the-fellowship-of-christian-athletes-a-love-cult-that-continues-to.html.

"What Are the Questions?" *motive* Magazine. Boston University School of Theology (February, 1955). http://sth-archon.bu.edu/motive/issues/1955_February/assets/basic-html/page-1.html#.

Williams, Duncan. *Trousered Apes: Sick Literature in a Sick Society.* New Rochelle, New York: Arlington House, 1971.

Wilson, Ernest (audio tape of remembrances). Collection 515, Papers of Ernest Wilson. Wheaton: Billy Graham Center Archives. https://archives.wheaton.edu/repositories/4/resources/538.

University Publications and Archival Ephemera

Marshall's Special Collections Department is a treasure trove of archival material (both physical and digital), including a range of publications (whether official university printings or material generated by various student groups), letters (whether confidential or public in their day), and a variety of "ephemera" (such a flyers and lecture notes). And the staff has been unfailingly gracious in bringing forth items for me to study in their confines. Rather than footnote the hundreds of quotes drawn from these sources, I give citation specifics in the flow of the narrative. They're integral to the story and obviate redundancy. Hence, the bibliography merely indicates the sweep of research.

Periodicals

The Campus Chimes. 1958–1961, 1964.

Catalogue. 1871–1872, 1876–1877, 1880–881, 1887–1888, 1889–1890, 1899–1900, 1900–1901, 1930–931

The Chief Justice. 1945, 1947, 1955–57, 1964, 1968, 1970–71, 1973–78.

Et Cetera. 1950, 1956, 1968, 1970.

Excelsior. 1914

Marshall Magazine. 1999–2000, 2008, 2010, 2018

Marshall University News. 2018.

Mirabilia. 1901, 1911, 1916–17, 1919, 1926–27, 1929, 1930

MU Newsletter. 1995

The Parthenon. 1921, 1924, 1926, 1928, 1933–36, 1938, 1967–1970, 1971, 2012, 2016–2017.

The Voice. 1967, 1970.

Correspondence and Other Items

Letters from President Stewart Smith, Dean Lillian Buskirk, Dean Harold Willey, Presbyterian campus minister Hardin King, First Presbyterian Pastor Andrew Bird, the West Virginian Human Rights Commission, and a donor, Mrs. C. B. Conner.

1956–1957 Student Christian Association Summary Report.

"Analysis of Unpaid (Regular) Pledges." Marshall College Student Christiaan Association Sponsors, Inc. (April 30, 1960.)

"Articles of Operations and Bylaws" for the Christian Community at Marshall. 1966.

Buskirk, Lillian Helms. Typescript of "Mood of the Campus," remarks delivered at the Symposium on Higher Education and Marshall (November 11, 1965.)

"Manual for Student Counselors in the Men's Residence Halls." 1961.

"One Hundred Years of Marshall College." Huntington: Centennial Committee, 1937.

"Student Participation in Religious Activities." A planning document in support of the fund-raising drive for the Campus Christian Center. 1961.

Utterback, William Irvin. A ten-cent pamphlet entitled "The Great Life Cycle: An Illustrated Presentation of the Past, Present and Future on the Bases of Scripture. Huntington: Gentry Brothers, 1927.